Prentice
Hall Press

Library of Congress Cataloging-in-Publication Data

Kaplan, Robbie Miller.
    How to say it in your job search : finding a job using power words, phrases, and
communication secrets in résumés, letters, and interviews / Robbie Miller Kaplan.
        p.   cm.— (TESTPREP curriculum activities library)
    ISBN 0-7352-0185-4
    1. Résumés (Employment)   2. Cover letters.   3. Employment interviewing.

HF5383.K364   2001
650.14—dc21   2001036349

© 2002 by Prentice Hall

Printed in the United States of America

10 9 8 7 6 5 4 3 2

ISBN 0-7352-0185-4

Attention: Corporations and Schools

Prentice Hall Press books are available at quantity discounts with bulk purchase for
educational, business, or sales promotional use. For information, pleasee write to: Prentice Hall Special Sales, 240 Frisch Court, Paramus, New Jersey 07652. Please supply:
title of book, ISNB, quantity, how the book will be used, date needed.

 Paramus, NJ 07652

http://www.phpress.com

To the memory of my mom,
Jean Miller,

whose loving spirit inspired me to reach for the stars

and

To my husband,
Jim,

whose love and support make everything possible

Acknowledgments

Many thanks to my husband, Jim, for his technical expertise, resources, and limitless support during the writing process.

A big thanks to my friend Wade Robinson who tirelessly and willingly supports every writing project.

I couldn't have completed this project without the generous help of my clients and Stephanie Barclay, Nancy Brock, Donna Dickinson, Mary Fairchild, Leia Francisco, Rita Kayn, Judy Lynch, Betty McManus, Mary Moore, David Nye, Stan Paul, Debbie Pivnick, Erika Schuetze, Nancy Sullivan, and Carla Vernon.

About the Author

ROBBIE MILLER KAPLAN is a trainer, writer, and practitioner with an expertise in job search techniques and career planning. She is a frequent speaker and lecturer for business, academic, community, association, and governmental organizations. She is the author of *Sure-Hire Résumés*, *Résumé Shortcuts*, *Sure-Hire Cover Letters*, *101 Résumés for Sure-Hire Results*, *The Whole Career Sourcebook*, and *Résumés: The Write Stuff* and a contributing author to the *Strong Interest Inventory Applications* and *Technical Guide*. She holds a Bachelor of Arts in English from George Mason University and has a management background with Xerox Corporation.

Contents

CHAPTER 3
Handling Résumés Electronically 91

PART TWO
Covering All Bases—Cover Letters

CHAPTER 7

Responding to Advertisements...........................135

CHAPTER 8

Sending Unsolicited Letters...............................151

CHAPTER 9

Getting a Little Help from a Friend—Networking and Referral Letters...169

CHAPTER 13
Preparing Letters of Resignation..213

Part Three
Making the Best Impression—Interviews

CHAPTER 14
Preparing for the Interview...223

CHAPTER 17

Concluding Your Job Search Successfully..........................275

Résumé Index by Occupation 285
Index 287

Why This Book
Is for You

Your job search success hinges not only on initial contact with employers, but also on written and verbal communications that link you to employers from the initial application through the all-important job offer.

The job search has become increasingly competitive, and leading edge technology has forever changed and complicated the process. It is hard enough to have your résumé stand out from a huge stack of résumés, but now you're competing with millions of résumés delivered by electronic mail, facsimile, the postal service, and posted out there in cyberspace.

Communication Tools for the Job Search

Oral and written communication skills are your secret weapons in outsmarting the pack and capturing an employer's attention. You'll use these strategic tools to clearly demonstrate your qualifications through your skill, style, and adeptness with words and nonverbal communications.

How to Say It in Your Job Search provides the latest communication techniques to help you persuade employers that you're a perfect match for the job. Along the journey, you'll find diagnostic self-tests to help you identify areas you can improve to enhance your employability.

The Secrets of Showcasing Your Strengths Through Résumés

The days of using one approach to résumé writing are long gone. Many employers now use computerized systems to scan résumés for key words, and a computer, not the employer, pre-selects the most qualified applicants. Other employers are requesting you to deliver your résumé electronically while some require you to complete online applications at their Web sites.

What hasn't changed is how job seekers avoid, dread, and struggle with writing their résumés. Writing about yourself is difficult. It's a challenge to summarize and articulate your professional life, accomplishments, contributions, and personal uniqueness. But you *must* have a résumé to look for a job. You need one now and you'll need one for the rest of your working life. Résumés can make or break your ability to find a job, get promoted, or make a career transition. That's why résumé writing is a skill that is critical to your long-term career success.

Part One will take the mystery out of traditional, scannable, and electronic résumés and teach you how to prepare, customize, and utilize these different résumé types to effectively market your credentials. Dozens of examples will inspire you to translate diverse occupations, qualifications, and experience levels into sure-hire résumés.

Cover Letters that Grab Attention

Many applicants spend considerable time producing their résumés, but when it comes to writing letters, these same people exert little thought or effort and simply dash off quick letters. In fact, the importance of letters to an effective job search campaign is often overlooked. The job market is too competitive to ignore a proven strategy that provides a direct link to employers. Part Two shows you how and why letters can attract positive attention, make a vital connection, and provoke the reader to learn more about you.

A wise job seeker crafts a different letter for almost every job search inquiry and scenario. Included here are the basics and characteristics of electronic, unsolicited, advertisement, referral, networking, thank-you, follow-up, offer acceptance/decline, and resignation letters. You'll find easy-to-follow instructions for each type of letter along with suggestions for solving bewildering situations. I'll show you how to make your letters sparkle through numerous examples, along with strategies to expedite and finalize your search.

Selling Yourself in Person

Once you sell yourself in writing, you'll learn how to nail the all-important job interview. Part Three lays the groundwork for a wide range of scenarios with tips on all facets of the interview. I'll demystify the research process and equip you for success with key strategies for advance preparation, references, nonverbal communications, answers to questions, what to ask, how to follow up, salary negotiations, and the final interview evaluation. You'll know which blunders to avoid and master the process to get you where you want to go.

It's all here—the ins and outs you need to navigate the job search with effective words that enhance your "hireability." Whether overcome with writing anxiety, too paralyzed to speak, or unsure of how best to present yourself, *How to Say It in Your Job Search* offers critical advice about oral, written, and nonverbal communications and useful models you can adapt and use through every stage of a successful job search. Good luck!

Robbie Miller Kaplan

PART ONE

Good Beginnings—
Résumés

Writing Your Best Résumé

1

Self-Test Your Savvy in Writing Your Résumé: How Good Are You at Marketing Yourself on Paper?

The following self-test is a tool to help you assess your readiness in writing and producing a résumé. The objective is not to get the highest score possible, but to pinpoint areas that you can strengthen to help you craft a résumé that will effectively market you for the jobs you seek.

1. I know I should always have an updated résumé. T/F __
2. It's okay to copy the format of a friend's résumé even if our work histories are different. T/F __
3. My first step in preparing my résumé is to identify my job search goals. T/F __
4. I can just hire professionals to write my résumé and they'll know the right words for my profession. T/F __
5. I should research the job requirements of positions that interest me. T/F __
6. I've seen many résumés begin with education, but my experience is my strongest asset so I should begin mine with experience. T/F __
7. There are specific qualities I want in a job so if I state these in a job or career objective, a prospective employer will know whether they are the company for me. T/F __

8. Employers like chronological résumés best.   T/F __

9. If I eliminate graduation dates from college on my résumé, employers won't discriminate against me.   T/F __

10. I don't want my current employer to know that I am looking for a job, so I will use a functional résumé that doesn't include a work history.   T/F __

11. I have lots of experience and demonstrated expertise and skills that I will highlight in a career or qualifications summary.   T/F __

12. I plan on using my résumé for several different jobs so I will include all my experience and let the hiring manager determine my suitability for openings.   T/F __

13. I have highly desirable technical skills and I should use a separate section to detail them.   T/F __

14. I should include every job and all my education and training on my résumé.   T/F __

15. My job titles don't really explain what I did so I should change them to make them more explicit.   T/F __

16. It's important that I detail the scope of my responsibilities and quantify and elaborate wherever possible.   T/F __

17. I'm not confident that I have an extensive vocabulary so I should use a synonym dictionary and a thesaurus to expand my word choice.   T/F __

18. I don't need to personally proof my résumé if my word-processing software has a spelling checker.   T/F __

19. I should carefully go through each position I've held and identify what I have accomplished.   T/F __

20. If my résumé demonstrates achievement, potential employers will know that I can perform at the same level for their organization.   T/F __

21. I'll let a trusted friend read my résumé, who will highlight word redundancies and errors for me.   T/F __

22. I should select my experience, education, training, publications, and certifications that showcase my qualifications for the positions I seek.   T/F __

23. I should include all specialized training to demonstrate my qualifications.   T/F __

24. My hobbies, interests, and sports show potential employers
    that I am well-rounded.   T/F __
25. I have a professional certification and should include
    the designation after my name to quickly establish my
    qualifications.   T/F __
26. It's okay if each experience sounds similar because all my jobs
    are similar.   T/F __
27. I shouldn't use my employer's electronic mail address.   T/F __
28. It's crucial that my résumé be error-free.   T/F __
29. I have no relevant paid experience, only volunteer experience,
    so I should put off preparing a résumé until I get some paid
    experience.   T/F __
30. It's okay to let someone copy my résumé. T/F __
31. My résumé must fit on one to two pages even though I have
    lots of work experience.   T/F __
32. I was nominated for an award and wasn't selected but I will
    include this information on my résumé because being
    nominated is an accomplishment.   T/F __
33. I have lots of volunteer experience with my church and
    should include it even though my work experience is enough
    to qualify me for the position I am seeking.   T/F __
34. I shouldn't use a résumé style sheet that comes with my
    word-processing software.   T/F __
35. I plan on balancing my résumé with boldface, bullets,
    uppercase, and lowercase.   T/F __

Total: _____

Score 1 point for each "True" response and 0 for each "False" response,
EXCEPT for questions 2, 4, 7, 9, 10, 12, 14, 15, 18, 24, 26, 29, 30, 33. *For
these questions only*, **subtract** 1 point for each "True" response. Record your
total. A score below +17 indicates that you would benefit from practicing the
résumé-writing techniques discussed in this chapter. (*Note:* It is possible to
have a negative score.)

Résumé Fundamentals

While technology has transformed the recruitment process, it has not changed the importance of résumés as the principal tool used to screen and identify job applicants.

No other document showcases your qualifications better than a well-written résumé. It gives the recipient a clear and detailed understanding of your credentials and enables you to effectively promote your strengths. You are in charge and you can package yourself and tailor your history to pursue any possibilities of interest.

Tip: Always keep your résumé updated so you'll be prepared to take advantage of any career or job opportunity.

You'll use résumés to communicate your qualifications in writing and sell yourself to prospective employers. But résumés have become much more than a personal marketing tool; if you are to attract an employer's attention you must write, format, and produce résumés that reflect how your experience, achievements, education, training, skills, and additional credentials match an employer's job requirements.

Résumés are just the first step in the job search process; effective résumés capture an employer's interest and lead to a personal meeting, an opportunity for you to sell yourself verbally during the job interview.

Types of Résumés

Once upon a time, job seekers created a résumé that was scanned by "human eyes." This all-purpose résumé may have been revamped in response to feedback during the search, but job seekers usually used this one résumé throughout their search.

In today's job market, résumés are a lot more complicated. Not only will you use a **traditional** résumé that will be scanned by "human eyes," but you will create **scannable** résumés that will be scanned into computer databases and read by "computer eyes."

If that isn't confusing enough, some employers will request **electronic** résumés that you transmit by electronic mail rather than delivering through the postal service or by facsimile machine.

If you are to compete effectively during your job search, you must learn how to create, produce, and use traditional, scannable, and electronic résumés. Traditional résumés are detailed in this chapter; you'll find all the information you need to craft scannable résumés in Chapter 2 and electronic résumés in Chapter 3.

Résumé Formats

There are two basic ways to format your résumé: either chronologically or functionally. Because your background and job objectives are unique, read through the following descriptions and the résumé samples in this chapter to choose a format that best positions you for the jobs you seek.

The chronological résumé summarizes your experience, education, and accomplishments in date order, beginning with the most recent and working backwards.

The chronological résumé is most appropriate when:

* You have held progressive job responsibilities or positions with increased accountability.
* Your work history follows a specific career path.

The chronological résumé is conventional and preferred by large corporations, public sector employers, and traditional industries such as banking, insurance, law, and accounting. See the chronological résumé example on page 28.

Four situations where the chronological format may not work:

1. Frequent job changes

Tip: Rather than listing several similarly titled jobs separately, minimize moves by using one job title and including the employers stacked under it, following each employer name with the actual employment dates.

---

2. Shifts in employment between industries or careers
3. Gaps in employment

Tip: Use separate experience sections with each work history in date order to bring clarity to shifts in employment or gaps; for example, organize "Accounting Experience" in one section and "Finance Experience" in another.

---

4. Change in careers

The functional résumé is an eclectic format with no hard or fast rules. It summarizes and emphasizes areas of experience or skills—the more specific the headings, such as compensation management, employee relations, benefits administration or marketing, sales, management, the better. Some individuals include a work history; others don't.

The functional résumé is most appropriate to:

- Help potential career changers demonstrate transferrable skills.
- Minimize repeated job changes or gaps in employment.
- Delineate skill areas when you have held one position for an extended period of time.

Many employers don't like functional résumés because they think the information is vague; it's hard for them to understand where you worked and what you accomplished. If this format suits you best, make sure you write descriptive, accomplishment-oriented statements. See the functional résumé example on page 50.

Nowadays, résumés have flexibility and it's possible to be creative by utilizing characteristics of both types of résumés:

- Combine functional experience areas within an introductory summary.
- Follow the chronological experience with a skills section organized functionally to break out transferrable or highly desirable skills.
- Separate a job with functional headings to emphasize specific work areas, break up a long entry, or bring definition to a position held for a long time. (See the résumé example on page 31.)

in Your Résumé

Your résumé should include some or all of the following sections:

1. Introductory summary (often called a career summary, qualifications summary, career history, summary of qualifications, profile, career profile, or professional profile)

Tip: Career or job objectives can be very limiting. Use them only if you have a very specific objective in mind and you don't think a summary will work for you.

2. Work history that includes jobs that relate to the positions you seek
3. Education, training, and professional development
4. Skills
5. Licenses and certifications
6. Awards and honors
7. Publications
8. Professional or community affiliations

Tip: Don't include addresses of employers, names of supervisors, reasons you left positions, your references, and personal information such as your weight, height, health, and marital or family status.

in Your Résumé

Your résumé should cast you in the best possible light. These detractors will take away from your credentials:

1. Stating you've been terminated, de-staffed, or laid off.
2. Noting that the job was unpaid. Experience is experience, whether paid or volunteer.
3. Personal statements or job objectives that tell employers what you want but not what you have to offer.
4. Misleading information such as making a statement that leads the employer to think you have completed college when you haven't.

5. A list of the five colleges you attended before completing your degree. You need to include only the college or university that awarded your degree.
6. College majors that have no relevance to the career you're pursuing. Just mention the degree.
7. Repeating the same job responsibility statements. Say it once and then include less and less information in following statements.
8. A list of hobbies. The only hobbies you should consider including are ones that have relevance, enhance your ability to do the job, demonstrate accomplishment, or are so unusual that they may trigger interesting conversation during an interview.

How to Say It in Your Résumé

If you're like most people, the prospect of writing a résumé may be overwhelming, especially if you have never done one or it's been a long time since the last update. Don't let the task intimidate you; the first step in the process is to relax. View the résumé as a puzzle; work on each section separately, and assemble the completed pieces.

- STEP 1: Make an outline of all the sections of the résumé that fit your credentials.

- STEP 2: Tackle one section at a time, working on the pieces that are easiest for you. The more you chronicle, the more confident you'll feel.

- STEP 3: People often find the experience section overwhelming. Before you begin, locate and organize your performance appraisals, job descriptions, job listings or advertisements, standards of performance, commendations, or letters of recommendation.

Tip: Read through job descriptions and postings on Web sites and the newspaper employment listings to cull information from similarly advertised and posted jobs.

- STEP 4: Chronicle your most recent job first; you'll have better recall. For this and all other jobs, craft an introductory statement that describes your primary responsibilities; demonstrate the scope and breadth, quantifying where possible.

  Example: Direct a worldwide operation marketing Internet products to corporate accounts.

  Example: Manage 30 sales and systems engineers in a rapid-growth technical environment with projected annual sales of $75 million.

  Example: Administer primary nursing care to multilingual and culturally diverse patients in a 10-bed high-risk Labor and Delivery Suite.

- STEP 5: Follow the introductory statement with additional facts of your key responsibilities.

  Example: Administer benefits and affirmative action programs. Ensure satisfactory employee relations by coaching, counseling, and providing ongoing career guidance.

- STEP 6: Once you have stated both your primary and key responsibilities, list your accomplishments. What did you achieve, how did you achieve it, and under what circumstances?

  Example: Achieved a 2.5% increase in annual sales, 3.5% greater than total ready-to-wear, despite company's Chapter 11 filing during this period.

Tip: Quantify whenever possible. When quoting figures for budgets and sales, use annual rather than monthly figures for more impressive results.

- STEP 7: Continue to describe prior jobs.

Tip: Use the most space to describe your most recent job and less and less space for each job in descending order.

- STEP 8: Once you have completed all of your work experiences, edit, rewrite, replace redundant words, and tighten prose.

- STEP 9: Proof your résumé several times to ensure 100 percent accuracy. Employers are known to toss out a résumé with one misspelled word or grammatical error. Ask a trusted friend or colleague to proofread it, too. Some people also find it helpful to proof from the bottom up.

Tip: It's easy to make mistakes spelling the names of computer hardware and software. Read through a current computer magazine and check your spelling in the product advertisements.

Fifty Words to Use in Your Résumé— and Why

You probably remember that you should use action verbs in your résumé but you may not remember why. The term "voice" refers to whether the subject acts or is acted upon. In active voice verbs, the subject (you) is the doer of the act. In passive voice verbs, the subject (you) is acted upon. Sentences with action verbs:

Pack more authority.

Use fewer words.

Are forceful, direct, and easier to understand.

Your résumé should be clear, concise, and contemporary using descriptive statements and the fewest words possible to detail the scope of your responsibilities and achievements.

So replace your passive voice verbs and add punch to your résumé with some of the following action verbs:

administer	assign	communicate	conduct	coordinate
analyze	build	compose	consult	craft
approve	collaborate	conceptualize	control	create

cultivate	expedite	integrate	participate	resolve
deliver	facilitate	investigate	penetrate	select
design	forecast	maximize	produce	set up
document	formulate	mentor	promote	team
enforce	foster	negotiate	recruit	track
evaluate	generate	operate	represent	train
expand	initiate	originate	research	write

Eight Redundant Words to Avoid— and Synonyms to Replace Them

Each of us has favorite words and we tend to state specific areas of responsibility within our occupations with a set of repetitive words. You'll eliminate redundancy and express yourself well if you use a thesaurus, synonym dictionary, or your online thesaurus while writing your résumé. Here are some overused verbs and a variety of synonyms you can use to replace them.

- develop—compose, create, design, generate, institute, set up
- establish—create, develop, institute, originate, set up
- identify—detect, disclose, establish, locate, pinpoint, reveal, uncover
- implement—accomplish, complete, execute, fulfill, launch, institute, perform, realize
- manage—administer, direct, guide, head, lead, oversee, supervise
- perform—conduct, execute, exercise, operate, produce
- prepare—administer, compose, develop, devise, produce
- provide—arrange, contribute, extend, furnish, implement, maintain, present, produce, supply

Fifty Verbs That Demonstrate Accomplishment

Employers have problems to solve and they want to hire employees who will have the skills and experience to quickly make a difference. Incorporate results-oriented verbs into your experience section and their meanings will add to your accomplishments:

achieved	entrusted	minimized	rated	revitalized
appointed	exceeded	overhauled	recognized	secured
attained	expanded	piloted	redesigned	selected
awarded	founded	positioned	reduced	spearheaded
conceived	granted	presented	reengineered	streamlined
consolidated	grew	produced	reorganized	surpassed
contributed	improved	progressed	resolved	transformed
customized	introduced	promoted	restored	tripled
doubled	invited	quadrupled	restructured	vitalized
enhanced	launched	ranked	revamped	voted

Phrases to Use in Your Résumé

actively recruit volunteer staff

arrange six monthly meetings

chaperoned a four-week environmental service project

co-founded *Phantom of the Opera* fan club

compete aggressively

contracted to teach reading, writing, listening, and speaking skills

create curriculum and deliver training programs

executed successful cablecasts of scheduled programming

extended superior quality service

generate sales and build client relationships

initiated and piloted a joint-venture alliance

launched an imaginative concept

selected from over 10,000 applicants nationwide

promoted after six months

provide full-service account management

selected to lead one of the most profitable districts

sold advertising in a five-state territory

top producer in invoiced revenue

Sentences to Use in Your Résumé

Added new clients and grew territory by 45%.

Awarded and completed a 14-week internship sponsored by The National Science Foundation and Northeastern University.

Built a competitive accounting staff by evaluating, redefining, eliminating, and creating positions to establish a cohesive and effective team.

Created corporate structure, wrote procedures, and managed all operational functions.

Critical member of management team that transformed a $5-million pre-tax loss in Fiscal Year 1998 to a $2.8-million pre-tax income in Fiscal Year 1999.

Direct multimillion-dollar international company with P&L responsibility and annual sales of $35 million.

Ensured accurate transmission of prerecorded and live material by playing and switching video sources according to set schedules.

Improved morale by designing interactive employee task forces.

Instructed aerobics classes and choreographed routines to meet multilevel student abilities.

Organized and processed written, statistical, technical, and dictated material for 50 users in eight departments.

Performed tests on a computer program that translated text from Spanish to English and English to Spanish.

Piloted unique conference, distance learning, and Intranet communications to deliver timely customer application-based training to 1,000 nationwide employees.

Received the organization's only letter of commendation from its largest customer.

Recognized as an industry leader for efficient, cost-effective, and quality services, dependability, and attention to detail.

Researched the effects of ultraviolet radiation on photosynthetic bacteria.

Retail sales representative for monthly upscale lifestyle magazine.

Paragraphs to Use in Your Résumé

Completed five-week full-time internship in outpatient orthopedic care. Treated sports-related injuries and chronic back pain.

Conceptualized and presented a business case and financial plan to support the launch of a strategic e-commerce business unit. Collaborated with senior management in the design and execution of long-range and operational plans.

Coordinated a $5-million food and beverage and service operation for business meetings and social functions at two airport properties. Oversaw ballroom set-up, ordered beverages and supplies, and directed events.

Developed and built new accounting practice. Increased active client number from zero to 400 and annual billings from zero to $.5 million within two years.

Directed all operations of an entertainment cruise ship. Hired, trained, and dismissed 70–80 seasonal employees.

Elicited support of divisional merchandise managers and store managers to drive incremental volume opportunities by store. Directed branch stores on presentation standards and key item intensification.

Estimate all phases of construction work and purchase services, materials, and equipment. Maintain the highest reputation for service and professionalism, producing high-quality detail on all finished projects.

Founded and managed a successful real estate corporation in the San Francisco metropolitan area, creating a niche in upper bracket sales. Grew business from a small office with 6 agents to 12 offices with 660 agents and annual sales of over $3.5 billion in 2000.

Handled teller operations for a busy savings and loan bank branch. Oversaw a daily cash drawer totaling over $30,000.

Manage operations for a 3,500-member private swim club with three pools, five tennis courts, and snack bar. Recruit, manage, schedule, and assign a staff of 20.

Market and sell guest rooms and convention space at a 752-room full-service hotel with 27,500 square feet of meeting space. Target new business to build revenue during traditional down periods. Manage a three-member support staff.

Oversaw housekeeping functions for 400 rooms and all public areas for a full-service hotel. Directed laundry operations, annually processing 2.5 million pounds, for two hotels with 790 guest rooms and all food and beverage linens.

Performed server duties at a high-volume specialty restaurant voted "Best New Restaurant 1999" by *Oh Savannah* magazine. Greeted guests and provided superior service to ensure a satisfying restaurant experience.

Managed retail activity for a diverse range of small, middle range, and key accounts within a five-state territory. Recruited, hired, trained, and directed a three-member sales support staff and nine part-time merchandisers.

Selected to research a coffeehouse venture on the Miami University campus. Co-interviewed students, staff, and faculty to determine venture appeal and desired services. Analyzed pastry, dairy, and vendor suppliers and costs and recommended findings to senior staff. Corporation launched two successful sites at the university based on recommendations.

Standardized training processes by instituting modular components that increased efficiency and reduced delivery time. Recognized for outstanding contributions by the corporate president.

Special Situations

~ *You've taken a position outside of your career plan and now you want to return to what you were doing previously.* You can state the experience that relates to the position you would now like to pursue in a first-experience section titled "Related Experience" and follow with all other experiences in another section titled "Professional Experience" or "Experience."

~ *You want a leadership role; your previous jobs were responsible but you didn't supervise anyone.* Search through your history to locate any leadership positions including those with professional affiliations or volunteer organizations. Chronicle these in a section titled "Leadership Experience," detailing how you supervised, oversaw, directed, recruited, or managed programs, staffs, events, or budgets. Quantify wherever possible.

~ *You have been working in one career field but recently completed training in another field and that is the one you would like to pursue.* Craft a strong summary that details your skills and overall qualifications, honing in on the new career. You might add functional areas and succeeding bullets in your summary. Try crafting an opening summary statement such as "Motivated performer with a technical educational background and a strong desire to repair, upgrade, and configure computers." Follow with education and include the training, certification, or recent degree. You may need to state actual courses to bolster your credentials. Identify any thread of skills, education, or experience to get a foothold into the new career area.

~ *You completed three years of your education and don't plan to finish.* State either three years towards a Bachelor of **, followed with the college, city, and state. Or state the college, city, and state followed by the actual years of attendance.

~ *You completed three years of your education and are currently pursuing completion.* Indicate "pursuing a Bachelor of **," followed with college, city, and state; "anticipate completion" and provide the year and month if applicable.

~ *You have no formal education.* If you've taken professional development courses, completed certification or professional studies, or participated in any training, include this information. It can go under an "Education" or "Training" heading. If you have no further training beyond high school, skip the education section altogether.

~ *You are unhappy with your current amount of responsibility and would like a position similar to one you once held.* You can downgrade your current job title and not emphasize such a wide scope of responsibility. Target your summary to match the requirements of the position you are now pursuing.

~ *You have worked as a consultant or have been running your own business and would like to work for someone else.* Always bear in mind that an employer seeks applicants who can solve their problems. Emphasize what you have accomplished that relates to your ability to contribute to another organization.

~ *You've heard of a curriculum vitae (CV) and don't know if you should use one.* A curriculum vitae is most often used by academic and health-care professionals. It is an extensive listing of certifications, licenses, education, training, board appointments, publications, presentations, and affiliations. Any professional with credentials that fall into these areas can use this format; for example, an association executive. See physician résumé example on page 47.

~ *You have been out of the work force for an extended period of time.* It is essential that you do your homework; determine what you would like to do and identify the job requirements. Upgrade your skills and experience by locating volunteer opportunities that bolster your qualifications. Volunteer activities are a wonderful way to update your skills, reenter the workforce, make a career transition, build a network, and bolster your confidence.

Organizing Your Résumé

Organize your résumé to quickly capture an employer's attention. You are unique and your format must reflect your personal strengths. Beware of copying a colleague's or relative's format; your résumé must be structured to showcase *your* attributes, not someone else's!

- STEP 1: Decide how best to order and arrange your sections. A background summary that details your experience, strengths, expertise, and skill areas is a great way to begin. It immediately demonstrates how your credentials match a job's requirements.
- STEP 2: Follow with areas of greatest strength: (1) If you are a recent graduate or have just completed education or specialized training, you might choose to follow with your education. (2) If your experience or special skills qualify you for the opportunities you seek, follow with the appropriate section. (3) Honors, awards, certifications, licenses, publications, and professional/community affiliations all follow last.

Tip: If you have designated certifications, for example, CPA, CIA, CISA, CMA, CFP, LSW, or RN, you should state these in the appropriate section but also include the initials after your name.

Here's how some people formatted their résumés:

Sheila K. has 12 years of progressive experience within the same organization and plans to stay within the same industry. She crafted a strong summary with bullets highlighting her skills. She followed with a chronological experience section that detailed her managerial accomplishments. Education, licenses, and professional affiliations came next.

Harry K. had 26 years of human resources management experience progressing to senior level. He planned to consult rather than seek a new position. He chose a functional format to avoid repetitiveness in his work experiences with functional headings from ten key areas of human resources such as training and development, succession planning, employee communications, and employee assessment. He wrote two to three descriptive bullets for each heading. Work history and education followed.

William S. just became an A+ Certified Technician. He prepared a bulleted qualifications summary that detailed his technical strengths and followed with his education and technical skills. His experience was included last as it supports his job objective but it is not in the same line of work.

Elizabeth C. recently completed her MSN, Adult Nurse Practitioner. She is currently a staff nurse and wants to land a nurse practitioner position. She led off with a profile followed by education, followed by a clinical affiliations section that highlighted her internships as a nurse practitioner and a nursing experience section. Credentials, licensure, and professional affiliations came last.

Producing Your Résumé

How will you attract employers who scan and evaluate hundreds of résumés? While content is essential to establish your credentials, it is your résumé's appearance that stimulates interest. Consider:

- Résumés should run between one and two pages. Make your choice on how the text fits and balances on the page(s). The only exception for a three-page résumé is an extensive listing of relevant publications.

Tip: You may want to consider formatting your résumé as a CV (see page 47) if you have extensive certifications, licenses, board appointments, affiliations, or presentations.

- Allow one-inch margins on the top, sides, and bottom of the page.
- Include your name and page two on the top of a succeeding page.
- Don't staple two résumé pages together; use a paper clip.
- Never produce two-sided copies of a two-page résumé.

Production steps:

- STEP 1: Choose a word-processing or desktop publishing software program that enables you to create and modify an attractive format that enhances your qualifications.
- STEP 2: Select a 10- or 12-point font. Think professional appearance but make your choice based on how the text will fit best on the page(s). Experiment with different fonts to balance the pages; try

Arial, Century Schoolbook, Book Antiqua, Bookman Old Style, and Times New Roman (only in 12 point).

Tip: Use two fonts; one for major headings and one for text. Choose one that is serif (such as Century Schoolbook, Times New Roman, Book Antiqua, Bookman Old Style) and one that is sans serif (such as Arial or Lucinda Sans).

- STEP 3: Use uppercase, bold, bullets, ruling lines, and indentations to emphasize targeted areas. Don't overload the résumé with special effects; use good judgment and view the résumé for balance and appeal.

Tip: Avoid underlining, parentheses, and dashes, which have a habit of stopping the eye.

- STEP 4: Begin your text (position titles, employers, degrees, and educational institutions) on the far left side, leaving dates for employment and education to follow text or right-hand justified. Too many people place their dates on the left—the area first scanned by employers.
- STEP 5: Balance your white space to maximize space while highlighting what you have to offer.
- STEP 6: Print copies either with laser or deskjet printers or a photocopier on $8^1/_2 \times 11$-inch 24-pound paper, 100-percent rag (best quality) or 25-percent rag (good quality).

Tip: Stationery supply stores and copy/print shops carry a wide range of paper. I prefer conservative colors and recommend white, off-white, buff, cream, ivory, or beige. Avoid grey and taupe colors and marbled, mottled paper, regardless of color; it's hard to read and photocopies poorly.

- STEP 7: Send your résumé in a 9×12-inch envelope so it will arrive unwrinkled.

Tip: Avoid using 14-point fonts for your name and headings. It overwhelms the résumé.

Sample Résumés

The following sample résumés cover 21 different occupations. They are arranged in alphabetical order as listed here.

Attorney

Auditor

Claims Representative

Collection Supervisor

Controller

Counselor

Development Specialist

District Sales Manager

Entrepreneur

Executive Recruiter

Fitness Manager

Human Resources Manager

Internet Manager

Meetings Manager

Nurse/Clinician

Physician

Publications Manager

Real Estate Sales

Retail Manager

Senior Executive

Telecommunications Manager

SHELDON T. GREEN
111 Brownville Court, Potomac, Maryland 20854
(301) XXX-XXXX   E-mail: SGreen@abc.com

PROFESSIONAL PROFILE

Attorney with an expertise in export and a solid background in import, customs, and anti boycott regulatory compliance. Extensive experience as regulatory compliance officer, export attorney, export manager, and compliance consultant with organizations in the private and public sectors.

EXPERIENCE

Eye Tech Corporation (ETC), Washington, D.C., 1989-present
Corporate Attorney, Trade Compliance Manager, Washington Trade Office

- Manage the global trade compliance program for the sixth largest domestic computer company. Focal point for organization-wide export, customs, import, and anti boycott regulatory compliance requirements.

- Direct Washington, D.C. trade office operations; administer export authorizations and represent ETC in industry association activities and before federal government agencies.

- Designated as Acting Export Counsel.

Key Accomplishments

- Created the international trade audit, operations review, internal investigation, incident management, and risk assessment procedures and implemented them in the U.S. and 40 wholly-owned foreign subsidiaries.

- Conducted and coordinated over 30 internal operations reviews and compliance investigations in 15 countries. Managed oversight of six U.S. government export audits and over 100 international on-site post shipment inspections resulting in no significant findings or sanctions.

- Administered successful export product and technical data licensing operations resulting in the authorization of over $50 million in sales and service revenue.

- Led an international team in the development and implementation of an Internet trade controls protocol.

- Directed three international project teams charged with driving trade operations cost reduction and process simplification goals; saved an estimated $500,000.

- As Secretary and Compliance Consultant to the Corporate Compliance Committee, influenced the creation of an Intranet site featuring Web-based corporate compliance inventory and assessment profiles, responsive to the Federal Sentencing Guidelines for Organizations.

- Presented over 40 trade compliance training and awareness sessions to senior business managers, trade personnel, internal audit staff, and corporate security officers.

U.S. Department of Commerce, Washington, D.C., 1983-1989
Director, Office of Export Enforcement Support

- Established and managed a new government office supporting export enforcement operations.

- Office grew from initial five employees and a budget of $200,000 to a staff of 32 and a budget in excess of $1 million.

- Member of foreign export control bilateral negotiation team.

- Periodic designation as Acting Deputy Assistant Secretary for Export Enforcement.

Office of U.S. Representative Susan Miller, Washington, D.C., 1979-1983
Staff Director

Heller, Cohen and Hoffman, PA, Lansing, Michigan, 1975-1979
Attorney

U.S. Navy, 1970 -1972
Naval Aviator

EDUCATION

J.D., University of Michigan Law School, Ann Arbor, Michigan, 1975

Completed course work for an **M.S. in Program Analysis**, Michigan Tech University, Houghton, Michigan

B.A., Michigan State University, East Lansing, Michigan, 1969

BAR MEMBERSHIP

Licensed Member, Michigan Bar

PROFESSIONAL AFFILIATIONS

National Commission on Corporate Compliance Standards

Electronic Industries Association

Chairman, Export Compliance Subcommittee

PAULA COX, CIA

102 Grant Avenue
St. Paul, Minnesota 55155
(612) XXX-XXXX

QUALIFICATIONS SUMMARY

Financial professional with extensive and progressive experience in financial institutions. Expertise in financial planning and analysis. Solid technical, auditing, leadership, training, interpersonal, and oral/written communication skills. Dedicated performer, willing to persevere to meet/exceed organizational objectives.

EXPERIENCE

National Bank Examiners, Minneapolis, Minnesota, 1992-present
Chief Auditor, 1996-present
Auditor, 1992-1996

- Promoted to direct complex, sensitive, and large-scale audits of savings banks within a six-state region.

- Coordinate and delegate assignments to auditing teams of two to four. Provide technical training and guidance; validate accuracy of workpapers and reports.

- Facilitate the resolution of audit deficiencies by collaborating with the institution's management team in the development of action plans and performance goals.

- Recommend solutions for troubled institutions; for example, merger, purchase, conversion, 208 assistance, or liquidation. Exercise decision-making authority for initiating administrative actions.

- Achieve exceptional results while training entry-level auditors during a six-month probation period. Utilize one-on-one instruction to prepare auditors, ensuring each auditor meets performance standards.

- Assume management responsibility on an as-needed basis during Supervisory Auditor's absences.

- Conduct in-depth pre-audit analysis of financial institutions with a primary focus on the size and quality of assets, portfolio management methods, accounting systems, risk determination, regulatory compliance, and deficiencies/issues addressed by prior audits.

Key Accomplishments and Projects

- Guided senior executives at mid-sized institutions through the development and implementation of new or enhanced operational systems, policies, and procedures. These initiatives succeeded in resolving serious and long-standing audit deficiencies, improving the financial position of these institutions.

- Led the distribution of new PC equipment (IBM Thinkpads) to the regional staff. Selected as one of two auditors to deliver training programs to over 110 auditors.

- Conducted field tests for the newly developed AIRES software application and all other in-house software programs. Worked closely with developers and programmers to resolve problems and enhance user options. Served as the lead trainer for regional staff.

- Detected, investigated, and facilitated the prosecution of several fraud cases.

State of Minnesota, Division of Financial Regulation, Office of the State Bank Commissioner,
St. Paul, Minnesota, 1986-1992
Financial Auditor Supervisor I, 1989-1992
Financial Auditor II and III, 1987-1989
Financial Auditor I, 1986

- Rapid promotions to direct, supervise, and appraise financial auditors conducting audits of financial institutions throughout the State of Minnesota. Established an annual audit plan, scheduled audits, and assigned auditors. Ensured overall compliance with regulations, determined financial conditions and stability, assessed quality of assets, and evaluated management performance.

- Wrote detailed reports of audit findings and recommendations for changes in management, operations, and procedures for regulatory compliance. Conducted entrance and exit interviews with top-level management.

Key Accomplishments and Projects

- Completed a seven-month special assignment investigating mortgage broker/banker complaints. Conducted extensive research and interviews to collect pertinent data and made final case resolutions. Developed the State's first-ever auditor program for the mortgage banking industry.

- Instrumental in the initial computerization of agency operations using personal computer systems for a variety of applications including spreadsheet analyses, database management, and word processing. Active in planning and implementing system upgrades, customizing existing programs, and leading user training/support.

Capital Investors Corporation, St. Paul, Minnesota, 1985-1986
Financial Services Representative, 1985-1986

- Sold a variety of financial services and investment products to individuals and small business owners in the Minneapolis/St. Paul area.

- Met with prospective clients to evaluate investment objectives and financial conditions. Followed through with the recommendations of appropriate products and accompanying profit projections. Built a strong reputation for honest and professional service.

EDUCATION

University of Minnesota, Duluth, Minnesota
M.B.A., selected for **Graduate Assistant Program**, 1984; **B.A., Business Administration, major in Accounting/Economics**, 1982

Professional Development; completed 24 Auditor Training Programs sponsored by the Institute of Internal Auditors

CERTIFICATION

Certified Internal Auditor (CIA)

HARRY T. CRANE
66 Oakdale Lane
Detroit, Michigan 48220
Work (313) XXX-XXXX   Home (313) XXX-XXXX

QUALIFICATIONS SUMMARY

Insurance professional with 14 years of progressive experience. Solid background and knowledge of all aspects of the insurance industry with a special interest in risk management. Exceptional analytical abilities and a proven record in resolving commercial and personal lines claims involving casualty and property.

EXPERIENCE

MIDWEST INSURANCE COMPANY, Detroit, Michigan
Senior Claims Representative, Claims Representative, 1996-present

Promoted to analyze, resolve, and settle casualty and property claims within the Detroit metropolitan area for the personal lines division of a leading insurance company.

Investigate liability in tort claims and successfully negotiate a range of settlement options including structured settlements.

Represent corporation in litigated cases. Select legal counsel and coordinate defense.

Consistently meet organizational goals of suit avoidance and economic settlement.

SOUTHWEST INSURANCE COMPANY, Phoenix, Arizona and Denver, Colorado
Senior Claims Representative, 1990-1996

Assessed and adjusted property and casualty claims for the Phoenix Claims Office and the Denver Claims Office.

Investigated liability claims and prepared recommendations for the resolution of a wide range of tort claims. Worked with private investigators, police, and witnesses.

Promoted to Senior Claims Representative in September 1993.

Presented "Southwest President's Award" in February 1992.

Won "Third Quarter Service Award" in 1990 and 1991.

UNIVERSAL INSURANCE COMPANY, Phoenix, Arizona
Claims Adjuster, 1987-1990

Investigated property insurance losses, analyzed policy coverage, estimated damage, and made cash settlements for personal and commercial lines of insurance coverage.

Selected to design a training curriculum for the position of multi-line office adjuster.

EDUCATION

B.A. in Liberal Arts, University of Michigan, Ann Arbor, Michigan, 1987

CERTIFICATION

Pursuing **Associate in Risk Management (ARM)**; passed two parts - anticipate sitting for third exam

SAMANTHA D. REED
12 Balmy Way, San Diego, California 92180
Work (619) XXX-XXXX Home (619) XXX-XXXX

QUALIFICATIONS SUMMARY

Collection professional with eight years of progressive experience. Effective manager, motivating staff to consistently exceed organizational objectives. Dedicated performer, willing to go the extra mile to meet aggressive goals.

EXPERIENCE

California Mutual, San Diego, California   1993-present

Collection Supervisor   1997-present

- Direct collections of outstanding consumer loans for the largest commercial lender in California. Manage a staff of 16 collectors; interview, hire, supervise, counsel, coach, and evaluate performance. Train staff on computerized collection systems.

- Establish biweekly and monthly goals for individual collectors and overall section to reduce delinquency and meet organizational performance targets. Monitor daily activities to ensure staff complies with standards.

- Execute collection efforts for uncollectible accounts. Evaluate, negotiate, and implement alternatives to resolve debt through counseling, loan settlements, interest rate reductions, asset disposal, third-party intervention, or charge off.

- Received "President's Award," 1999.

- Awarded "Outstanding Section Supervisor," February, March, April, May, June, and July 1998.

- Received "Sustained Superior Performance Award," 1998.

Senior Credit and Collection Coordinator   1993-1997

- Promoted five times within three years based on outstanding collection achievements.

- Assumed senior assignment ranked in the bottom third and within one month, recognized as top branch performer.

- Persistently approached each outstanding debt and skillfully created an individualized collection strategy that effectively resolved delinquencies.

- Awarded "Certificate of Recognition for Sustained Superior Performance," 1995.

EDUCATION

Bachelor of Arts in English, San Diego State University, San Diego, California, 1992

ROBIN A. ESCOTT
46 Dante Boulevard, Eastchester, New York 10709
(914) XXX-XXXX E-mail: Rescott@aab.com

CAREER HIGHLIGHTS

Seasoned professional with progressive experience in all aspects of accounting and financial management. Proven record in delivering quality accounting services, consistently meeting established deadlines. Proficient with Microsoft Office products and spreadsheet programs.

EXPERIENCE

Megamedia Incorporated, New York, New York, 1970 - 2001

CONTROLLER, 1990 - 2001

- Directed financial and accounting functions for a Fortune 500 media corporation with annual revenue of $300 million. Prepared and administered annual operating budget of up to $250 million.
- Managed a staff of eight performing daily operations within accounts payable, accounts receivable, payroll, cashiering, and billing. Assisted with annual internal and external audits.
- Produced and presented monthly and annual financial statements to senior executive staff.
- Established credibility and developed positive long-term relationships that supported internal and external customers by fostering teamwork and collaboration.
- Built master files for general ledger to interface with client billing as part of organization-wide computer system conversion.

DIRECTOR OF ACCOUNTING, 1982 - 1990

- Managed accounting operations and three-member staff. Prepared journal entries for posting to general ledger for preparation of monthly close and financial statements.
- Ensured all federal and state monthly, quarterly, and annual taxes filed within specified time frames.
- Balanced and reconciled employee benefits, including vacation, sick leave, and retirement, and submitted invoices for monthly payment.
- Initiated and implemented payroll time and attendance system and direct deposit for employee paychecks.
- Streamlined the accounts payable process, facilitating quicker payments that increased purchase discounts 50%.

CHIEF ACCOUNTANT, 1978 - 1982

- Prepared journal entries, amortizations, and other schedules for monthly financial statements to meet financial reporting guidelines. Balanced and reconciled all bank accounts.

ACCOUNTANT, 1970 - 1978

- Acquired solid accounting and financial background and developed proficiency with computerized operations.

EDUCATION

A.S. in Accounting, Westchester Community College, Purchase, New York

KATHLEEN PORTER

15 Coastal Highway
Work (206) XXX-XXXX

Seattle, Washington 98121
Home (206) XXX-XXXX

CAREER SUMMARY

Experienced counselor in higher education with expertise in the fields of career/life planning, professional development, and community college education.

EDUCATION

Ed.D., 1999, University of Seattle, Seattle, Washington. Counselor Education with cognate area in Higher Education Administration. Awarded graduate assistantship as Coordinator of Personal & Career Development Center in the School of Education. Dissertation assessed the professional development needs of community college counselors in Washington.

M.S., 1973, Gonzaga University, Spokane, Washington. Concentration in Personnel Services and Counseling. Awarded a graduate assistantship as Assistant Director of Placement for the university.

B.A., 1971, Walla Walla College, College Place, Washington. Major in Social Science and Psychology.

PROFESSIONAL EXPERIENCE

Associate Professor/Coordinator of Off-Campus Counseling Programs
SOUTH SEATTLE COMMUNITY COLLEGE (SSCC), Seattle, Washington, 1976 - present

Administer off-campus services for military personnel at Fort Henry and Headquarters, U.S. Navy.

Provide counseling and other student support. Supervise SSCC staff responsible for admission and records, student payments, military tuition assistance, and publicity. Coordinate 40 course offerings for 800+ students per semester and other SSCC activities with military education centers.

Coordinate career and life planning programs. Provide academic, career, and personal counseling to students and community members in groups and individual sessions.

Develop and teach three-credit psychology course to facilitate career and life planning processes.

Selected Accomplishments

Professional Development

♦ Designed a system for equitable disbursement of human resource development funds totaling $40,000 as chair of faculty HRD committee. 1998 - 2000.

♦ Appointed to the Chancellor's Professional Development Task Force to design a faculty professional development program for the Seattle Community College Symposium. 1997 - 2000.

♦ Wrote proposals regarding disbursement of faculty tuition assistance and interview policy as chair of campus faculty professional development committee. 1996 - 1999.

Career/Life Planning

- Co-authored *Career Directions: A Guide for Career/Life Planning* (4th edition) published by Smith-Hart, written to facilitate the career/life development of the adult student. This text is used throughout the United States and Canada.

- Designed and implemented a comprehensive career and life planning service for students, faculty, and the community including job fairs, workshops, classes, and counseling. Trained counselors and interns to facilitate classes and workshops. 1976 - present.

- Obtained three grants totaling $45,000 to evaluate effectiveness of the counseling services, write career/life materials for adults, and link community resources with the community college. 1992, 1995, 1998.

- Presented and consulted at local and national professional, academic, and community conferences on topics including Team Building Using the MBTI, Increasing Self-Esteem, Career Development for the 21st Century, and Adult Life Transitions. 1976 - present.

RELATED EXPERIENCE

Director of Student Affairs, Seattle University, Seattle, Washington, 1974 - 1976

Assistant Director for Placement, Gonzaga University, Spokane, Washington, 1973

Admission Counselor, Walla Walla College, College Place, Washington, 1971 - 1973

PROFESSIONAL CERTIFICATIONS

National Certified Counselor (N.C.C.)

National Career Counseling Certification (N.C.C.C.) from National Board of Certified Counselors, an affiliate of the American Counseling Association

PROFESSIONAL AFFILIATIONS

American Counseling Association

Washington Community College Association

Washington Counselor Association

Washington College Placement Association

RACHEL W. ANTHONY
12 Laurel Lane, Columbus, Ohio 43200
Work (614) XXX-XXXX   Home (614) XXX-XXXX

CAREER HIGHLIGHTS

Enthusiastic and dedicated development specialist with a solid background in project management, event planning, and fund-raising. Exceptional leader with a proven record in recruiting, training, and motivating large-scale teams for fund-raising and community events. Excellent communication and interpersonal skills.

EXPERIENCE

American Society for Diseases, Columbus, Ohio   1990 - present
DEVELOPMENT SPECIALIST   1995 - present

- Organize and implement major multisite fund-raising projects, *Celebrate Life* and *Rose Day*, that raise over $.5 million annually for a nonprofit organization. Skillfully manage budgets to ensure expense ratios do not exceed organizational requirements.

- Recruit, train, and support volunteer leadership teams; present motivational speeches to corporations, schools, hospitals, and civic groups that consistently generate hundreds of volunteer participants.

- Assist with the design and format of meetings; define the agenda, invite speakers and presenters, coordinate space and menus with hotels, and arrange the logistics.

- Serve on a regional advisory team to standardize procedures and incentives for major fund-raising events in a five-state area. Contribute to the design of promotional materials and co-plan and deliver training programs to staff and volunteers.

- Mentor and conduct one-on-one training for all new fund-raising staff members.

SENIOR AREA DIRECTOR, AREA REPRESENTATIVE   1990 - 1995

- Promoted to manage fund-raising projects, on-site prevention and early detection programs, and board management for a two-county area.

- Conceptualized and managed community-based fund-raising events. Recruited and led volunteer teams to plan and organize local events that repeatedly generated financial support.

- Promoted national prevention and early detection events at the local level. Interacted extensively with two 40-member boards of directors.

The Peterson Group, Cincinnati, Ohio   1987 - 1990
PERSONNEL CONSULTANT   1987 - 1990

- Consulted with clients to identify staffing needs. Prepared job descriptions, wrote and placed recruitment advertisements, screened resumes, and qualified candidates. Interviewed applicants, arranged applicant interviews with clients, and negotiated salaries.

- Prepared and administered placement bills. Followed up with clients to ensure satisfaction with placement and built relationships for future placement needs.

EDUCATION

Bachelor of Science in Education, University of Cincinnati, Cincinnati, Ohio   1987

STEPHANIE R. HERNANDEZ
101 SW 79th Avenue, Miami, Florida 33170
Home (305) XXX-XXXX Work (305) XXX-XXXX E-mail: SRH@abc.com

PROFESSIONAL PROFILE

Top sales performer with exceptional selling skills and a proven record in developing entrepreneurial organizations, motivating staff to achieve results. Enthusiastic team player with an aggressive and persistent approach to identifying and closing sales. Expertise in building business relationships, customer loyalty, and establishing long-term business partnerships.

EXPERIENCE

Devlin Corporation, Miami, Florida
DISTRICT SALES MANAGER, 1995-1998, 1999-present

- Launched and marketed a new outsourcing service in a five-state territory for the leading national medical records correspondence company. Built a successful customer base with annual revenue in excess of $1.3 million.

- Negotiate and administer contracts for outsourcing services with large health-care organizations, medical institutions, and state and federal agencies including Medical College of Florida, Miami-Dade Hospital, Gold Coast Medical Center, Tampa Bay Medical Center, and Department of the Army.

Sales Achievements

- Consistently exceed sales quotas through effective direct marketing campaigns and utilization of strategic selling techniques.

- Ranked #1 out of 11 sales representatives nationwide, January-June 1998.

- Ranked #3 nationwide for sales revenue, Fiscal Year 1997.

- "Achievement Award Winner," 1996; highest monthly revenue for radiology program, Fiscal Year 1996.

- Sold the largest radiology customer in 1996.

- Established an innovative referral program instituted nationwide.

- Winner, "Highest Revenue Award," 1996 sales training class.

New Venture Software, Charlotte, North Carolina
ACCOUNT EXECUTIVE, 1998-1999

- Piloted five Enterprise Resource Planning (ERP) software applications in a multistate territory for a newly formed company. Penetrated the health-care industry and introduced applications to a large legal practice.

- Negotiated and sold the first system out of a training class of ten sales representatives nationwide.

- Sold two major systems to hospitals within initial nine months.

Telecommunications Inc., Atlanta, Georgia
MARKET MANAGER, 1994-1995

- Established sales operations for a leading cellular manufacturer/distributor in AT&T Mobile's Atlanta marketplace. Hired, trained, and built a successful direct sales staff with annual revenue exceeding $1.1 million.

- Created distribution channels; instituted major accounts for national associations and large corporations, accounting for 67% of revenue.

- Achieved 131% over quota for 1995. Realized above-average return on sales through detailed financial analysis and management of P&L statements. Gross profit leader among southern markets.

- Designed and coordinated innovative promotional strategies at sporting events and retail operations. Set up and managed inside retail kiosks with national organizations.

- Increased gross profit 29% per sale by creating new product packaging.

- Selected "Best Market Manager" for 1st and 2nd Quarter, 1995.

- Winner, 1994 4th Quarter sales contest.

Laneer Corporation, Atlanta, Georgia
ACCOUNT EXECUTIVE, 1993-1994

- Cultivated and managed national territory for new start-up corporation marketing information systems to major cellular communication companies including GTE Mobilnet, SBC, and McCaw Communications.

- Developed financial models used in proposals with major cellular companies.

- Initiated and implemented a new service strategy resulting in 10% of revenue.

- Successfully executed marketing campaign with ADR voice mail and fax deliveries.

EDUCATION

EMORY UNIVERSITY, Atlanta, Georgia
M.B.A. in Marketing, 1995
B.S., Business and Finance, 1992

COMPUTER SKILLS

Proficient in Windows 98, Microsoft Office, contact manager software applications, Internet research.

TED E. SPELLING
9112 Hilltop Street, San Francisco, California 94117
Work (415) XXX-XXXX Home (415) XXX-XXXX

PROFESSIONAL PROFILE

Dynamic senior executive with outstanding achievements in marketing and sales. A resourceful leader, willing to take risks and pursue new ideas while exceeding aggressive financial goals.

Visionary, skillfully increasing business volumes and penetrating new markets. Proven record in identifying opportunities, organizing resources, and executing plans. Exceptional interpersonal and presentation skills.

EXPERIENCE

Founder, President, TES Cash, San Francisco, California, 1996 - present

- Founded one of the first noninstitutional retail ATM deployment companies. Established distributorships with key equipment manufacturers and three of the largest ATM gateway processors. Marketed and negotiated nationwide merchant agreements to deploy over 300 ATMs in strategic hospitality, transportation, entertainment, and retail locations within the initial six months.

- Recruited, hired, developed, and built a nationwide team of 40 professional sales representatives.

Selected Accomplishments

- Created a unique partnership investment program that reduced capital expenditures by 90%, decreased corporate operating capital requirements by 75%, facilitated rapid expansion, and dramatically increased corporate earnings to over $1 million annually.

- Originated innovative marketing programs directed to businesses and users that captured a large market share and increased nationwide machine placements, applications, and ATM usage despite an initial hostile environment.

- Persistently cultivated and built relationships and alliances with non-ATM companies that opened and penetrated new markets.

- Instituted a round-the-clock in-house monitoring system and engineered the logistics for an internal cash fulfillment program, ensuring 98% operability and unparalleled service response time.

- Pioneered a dynamic ATM-based advertising program that branded machines, sold products, marketed business services, and generated new revenue sources.

- Introduced an in-house service and maintenance program that cut costs 75% and significantly reduced installation time while improving response time and service delivery.

Owner, Sales Manager, Western Finance, San Francisco, California, 1996

- Opened independent branch office for one of the top 25 nationwide debit and credit card processing companies. Recruited and managed a sales team.

- Within one year, signed over 100 merchants, providing equipment and equipment financing to new customers.

- Built a market presence, penetrated new business, and expanded market share by prospecting, cold calling, utilizing direct mail programs, networking, and participating with professional and trade associations. Formed networking groups that generated increased viable leads.

- Designed marketing materials and systems that quickly acclimated the sales force, educated the customers, and rapidly increased sales. Created time-saving sales collaterals that simplified the sales cycle and shortened sales interactions.

Sales Manager, Golden Gate Corporation, San Francisco, California, 1995 - 1996

- Revamped marketing focus and increased credit/debit card sales 500% within the initial month.

- Significantly built sales productivity by spearheading expansion into new states and regions, recruiting district managers, and growing the sales force.

- Instituted a corporate-wide training program to enhance sales performance.

- Originated a sales program that increased corporate sales by qualifying individual businesses that didn't fit approval criteria for group programs.

Sales Manager, Northern California Finance, San Francisco, California, 1994 - 1995

- Recruited and trained a results-oriented sales organization that quickly led the credit and debit card market in sales. Opened offices in New Jersey and Richmond and expanded the sales team.

- Participated in developing strategic plans to grow the organization, increase deal production, and implement compensation and bonus programs that strengthened morale. Generated a telemarketing incentive program that dramatically improved lead quality.

- Created the infrastructure that tracked and expedited contracts and shortened the installation cycle. One of three sales executives out of 90 selected to represent the company at vendor conferences.

Owner, Wearables Unlimited, San Luis Obispo, California, 1986 - 1995

- Launched a successful apparel company in a competitive industry. Created, manufactured, and sold customized novelty products throughout the United States. Opened markets through direct mail, cold calling, and prospecting.

- Conceptualized original designs and hired diverse artisans to produce, colorize, and prepare designs for production. Generated extensive publicity and media attention by promoting product uniqueness.

- Sold over 26 lines of apparel and acquired contracts with large retail outlets, special event planners, specialty stores, academic institutions, and social groups.

- Managed logistics for entire production and distribution of 400,000 apparel items annually.

EDUCATION

B.S. in Finance, California Polytechnic State University, San Luis Obispo, California, 1991

ROBERTA A. HARRINGTON
8221 Park Terrace, Wilmington, Delaware 19898
(302) XXX-XXXX

PROFESSIONAL PROFILE

Top sales performer in IT business development and recruitment, successfully meeting the challenges of a competitive and fast-paced environment. Skilled in establishing partnerships, meeting client needs, and consistently closing sales.

- Built sales revenue through superior customer service, repeat business, and referrals.

- Launched an innovative idea for a restaurant business from inception through profitability.

EXPERIENCE

Brown Group, Wilmington, Delaware
EXECUTIVE RECRUITER, 1999-present

- Selected to cultivate and develop new business for a technology staffing firm.

- Recruit top talent in the technology field for opportunities in e-commerce, SAP, Oracle, and enterprise resource planning (ERP) technologies.

Executive Recruiters of Baltimore, Baltimore, Maryland
ACCOUNT EXECUTIVE, 1997-1999

- Successfully recruited talent for start-up companies and Big-five firms that met client requirements by identifying corporate needs and culture, facilitating strategic and tactical talent acquisition.

Selected Accomplishments

- Nationally ranked in the top 25% nationwide over 5,000 account executives in 1998.

- Recruited eight top SAP HR Payroll consultants for HR-specific consulting firm, contributing to over $2.5 million new revenue, a 25% growth over nine months.

- Awarded "Biller of the Year" in 1998.

- Recruited key players to build a niche technology division for a Big-five firm.

- Ranked #1 in East Region in revenue for 1997.

- Recruited five technical consultants and an e-commerce practice lead that helped a start-up firm grow from $1.3 million to over $5 million, a 500% revenue increase within one year.

- Built an extensive database of over 5,000 technology contacts and resumes over the last three years to access top talent in each of the technology fields.

Valley Inn, Newark, Delaware
PARTNER, 1996-1997

- Co-founded casual-oriented restaurant, emphasizing 100% customer satisfaction. Interviewed, hired, trained, motivated, and managed a staff of ten associates and one manager.

- Cultivated relationships with existing and new vendors; obtained the best-quality food and beverage products at the lowest prices, increasing profitability.

- Established and monitored profit and loss, budgets, forecasts, and inventory control.

- Instrumental in promoting restaurant through advertising and public relations programs. Planned, designed, and placed newspaper ads and radio spots.

- Grew monthly restaurant sales to $25,000. Sold restaurant for a profit within 12 months.

- Recognized as the "Rookie of the Year" in the restaurant business, *Newark's Best* magazine, November 1996.

Maryland Mutual, Baltimore, Maryland
SALES AGENT, 1995-1996

- Sold life insurance programs, annuity contracts, and accident and health insurance to individual and corporate clients.

- Educated clients on policy features, prices, and coverage. Grossed over $500,000 in annual sales.

Miller Enterprises, Inc., Newark, Delaware
ASSISTANT MANAGER, 1990-1995

- Effectively coordinated and maintained sales and marketing program for propane and related products. Recruited, trained, and supervised staff.

- Identified and targeted potential customers, analyzed and tracked sales trends, and recommended merchandise selection.

EDUCATION

Bachelor of Arts, major Government and Politics, minor History, 1994
University of Delaware, Newark, Delaware

COMPUTER SKILLS

Proficient in Windows 98, Microsoft Word, Excel, PowerPoint, and the Internet.

LOUISE BERRY
45 Magnolia Street, New Orleans, Louisiana 70115
(804) XXX-XXXX

QUALIFICATIONS SUMMARY

Goal-oriented and enthusiastic professional with a solid background in marketing, promotions, and event planning. Excellent communicator, dedicated to achieving optimal organizational performance.

EXPERIENCE

Bourbon Street Sport and Health, New Orleans, Louisiana
Program Coordinator, **Senior Fitness Supervisor**, 1999 - present

- Rapid promotion to direct programming for a 2,200-member health and wellness club. Conceptualize, initiate, and launch programs that educate members, enhance membership, and improve profitability.

- Create, approve, and schedule an annual calendar of monthly events; prepare and administer annual and event budgets. Plan seasonal party and silent auction for 600 attendees.

- Manage a staff of eight; assign event responsibilities, establish promotion deadlines, and conduct monthly meetings. Recruit and hire speakers and trainers for special events.

- Design innovative promotional materials that consistently attract attendance and increase club retention rate. Produce a monthly activities calendar for members and contribute quarterly programming articles for club newsletter.

- Train and assist members on exercise equipment through assessments and programs. Deliver customer-focused service to ensure member satisfaction.

- Assume management responsibilities on a daily basis. Active role in membership sales; conduct club tours for prospective members and prepare membership paperwork.

- Selected "Employee of the Quarter," 1st Quarter 1999.

United States Capitol Police, Washington, D.C.
Health and Fitness Intern, September - November 1998

- Trained police officers, Containment and Emergency Response Team, and recruits; performed fitness assessments, prescribed exercise, and instructed classes. Taught lifestyle modification and counseled on risk-factor prevention.

- Created promotional brochures on low-back exercises and stretching, developed a video on proper use of exercise equipment, and piloted a walking club.

EDUCATION

Georgetown University, Washington, D.C.
Bachelor of Science in Exercise and Sports Science with honors, December 1998
Women's Varsity Swim Team, 1994 - 1998
Women's Swimming Team Captain, 1997 - 1998

CERTIFICATIONS

National Sports Performance Association; Certified Conditioning Specialist (CCS)
American Red Cross; CPR Certified, First Aid Certified, Lifeguard Training Certification

TONY FORTUNE

76 Grand Avenue
Houston, Texas 77058
Work (713) XXX-XXXX   Home (713) XXX-XXXX

PROFILE

Over 15 years of demonstrated success in Organizational Development, Management Development, Human Resource Management, Training, and Consulting Services. Specialize in spearheading management and organizational development initiatives that improve the internal capability to respond to strategic challenges driven by customer and business requirements.

EXPERIENCE AND RESULTS

Manager, Management and Organization Development, 1997 - present
ABC TECHNOLOGY, Houston, Texas

Lead and guide business units in the strategic planning, design, development, implementation, and evaluation of core systems, practices, and curriculum.

- Established company-wide team and individual development planning system including process, tools, curriculum, train the trainer, and certification methodology.

- Created, developed, and delivered line and mid-management training and organization improvement programs for client groups. Training replicated companywide with internal demand for products and tools up 75%.

- Directed task force initiative to institute company-wide comprehensive electronic training tracking system.

- Led cross-operational task force to design and set up company-wide PC-based development planning and organization information software system. 75% of business units are pursuing access.

- Selected to consult/advise the program management council on the plan, design, development, implementation, and evaluation of program management quality-improvement initiatives.

- Established and led cross-organization team in the design and pilot of a development center concept. Centers will double in one year due to favorable response.

- Designed and piloted first company-wide orientation/assimilation process including facilitator guide and employee information guides.

41

HRD Specialist, 1992 - 1997
  XYZ ELECTRONICS, Houston, Texas

Led region in the strategic planning, design, development, execution, and evaluation of core systems, practices, and curriculum.

- Initiated, developed, and facilitated the annual offsite strategic planning and team development for executive management.

- Directed regional implementation of employee surveys, performance management system, succession planning, high-potential programming, and regional development planning.

- Designed and delivered various training and development programs and curriculum in change management, cross-functional team development, performance improvement, and management and leadership assessment methodology.

Independent HR Consultant, 1988 - 1992

Provided consulting services in cross-agency program planning, business planning, team development, instructional design, and curriculum development to private and public sector clients.

County Resource Specialist, 1981 - 1988
  LOS ANGELES COUNTY, Los Angeles, California

Piloted liaison role between Los Angeles County Board of Education and special educators, providing a full range of staff development services.

EDUCATION

M.A., Counseling Psychology, Rice University, Houston, Texas, 1994

B.S., Education, Pepperdine University, Malibu, California, 1980

HONORS/AWARDS

ABC Technology Award for Outstanding Performance, 1999
XYZ Electronics Superior Performance Awards, 1995, 1996
XYZ Electronics Award for Outstanding Achievement, 1994

PROFESSIONAL AFFILIATIONS

American Society for Training and Development
National Social Sciences Honor Society

HOWARD DIAMOND
6772 Plantation Lane, Atlanta, Georgia 30341
(404) XXX-XXXX   E-mail: howard.diamond@abc.com

QUALIFICATIONS SUMMARY

Versatile technical professional with progressive experience in diverse industries. Proven record in improving business operations through the application of Intranet/Internet technology. Exceptional communicator, easily interacting with diverse professionals, clients, and staff members.

EXPERIENCE

EFG International, Atlanta, Georgia
MANAGER, INTRANET APPLICATIONS, 1998 - present

- Manage the development and delivery of Internet technology for domestic and global business units within the EFG enterprise. Facilitate Web-based solutions for EFG business problems by building teams of internal technical professionals and third-party developers.

- Consult with departments to identify Web-based applications that improve productivity, expedite work flow, reduce expenditures, and replace existing processes. Analyze current practices, generate potential solutions with Web technology, and introduce outside experts to design applications. Coordinate application development with technical staff to ensure integration with existing systems.

- Manage administrative and development teams for the enhancement and maintenance of the corporate Intranet.

- Market Web technology to showcase how Intranet solutions enhance domestic and international business performance.

Peachtree Bank, Atlanta, Georgia
VICE PRESIDENT, TECHNICAL OPERATIONS, 1995 - 1997
ASSISTANT VICE PRESIDENT, TECHNICAL OPERATIONS, 1993 - 1995
TECHNICAL MANAGER, 1992 - 1993

- Rapid promotions to direct technical operations for headquarters and 22-branch network of a regional bank.

- Oversaw implementation and management of telecommunications networks, data processing, and technical support to apply technology in the development of leading services and products.

- Conducted strategic analysis and recommended purchase of hardware, capital equipment, and dataprocessing outsourcing.

- Introduced and designed Web technology including an Internet presence, electronic mail services, and electronic commerce.

L&N International, Augusta, Georgia
BUSINESS ANALYST, 1991 - 1992

- Analyzed production of two major manufacturers. Wrote reports that contrasted current construction to historical trends to identify efficiencies and deficiencies. Delivered final report to a wide range of audiences. LAN Administrator (CNA) for Novell 3.X network.

EDUCATION

Bachelor of Science, Business Administration, Emory University, Atlanta, Georgia, 1991

SUZANNE SNYDER

15 Wiehle Avenue, Reston, Virginia 22090 Work (703) XXX-XXXX Home (703) XXX-XXXX

SUMMARY OF QUALIFICATIONS

Experienced meeting planner with solid experience organizing and managing all aspects of meetings and conventions including workshops, symposia, and exhibitions for organizations in the public and private sectors.

- Establish and implement conference and meeting services. Assist with the design and format of a meeting, define the agenda and attendance, select and negotiate the site, and invite speakers and presenters.
- Coordinate and organize volunteer help, process registrations, design and develop promotional and program materials, and recruit and supervise staff.
- Expertise in delivering quality projects under budget. Recognized specialist in transforming conceptual ideas into successful events.

EXPERIENCE

MEETINGS MANAGER, Snyder & Associates, Reston, Virginia, 1996 - present

Plan, manage, and implement all phases of meeting planning for a variety of clients. Provide services in budget development and financial management, on-site supervision, and logistical management.

- Orchestrated travel, hotel, accommodations, intricate meeting formats, exhibit programs, poster sessions, elaborate food and beverage functions, on-site production, and associated equipment for an annual scientific conference with two major groups of 500 meeting simultaneously.
- Conducted on-site management for a series of four seminars for 150 attendees sponsored by a major oil company.
- Coordinated logistics and registration procedures for a six-month series of training courses for 1,100 employees of a large federal government contractor.
- Managed a fee-paid technical conference for 200 attendees sponsored by a major software company.

CONVENTION MANAGER, American Association of Manufacturers, Reston, Virginia, 1992 - 1996

Established convention services department. Planned, developed, and executed all pre-convention, on-site, and post-convention activities, and logistics for annual convention of 1,200 attendees.

- Assisted in educational programming for the convention; reviewed proposals and selected presenters.
- Negotiated and managed airline travel for staff, officers, and convention participants.

MEETINGS MANAGER, American Society of Managers, Washington, D.C., 1988 - 1992

Organized, promoted, and managed complex formats for biannual meeting attended by over 2,400 participants, delivering optimal results under budget.

- Managed all functions of 75 booth exhibitions.

EDUCATION

Bachelor of Arts in English, The George Washington University, Washington, D.C., 1985

American Society of Association Executives: Effective Convention Management, 1994

Meeting Planners International: Meeting Management, 1992

HEATHER FRY

88 Cherry Tree Lane, Denver, Colorado 80217
Home (303) XXX-XXXX Work (303) XXX-XXXX

QUALIFICATIONS SUMMARY

Experienced clinician with a solid background in hospital and clinical settings. Independent and team player, working productively with individuals at all organizational levels. Adaptable and effective in high-demand, constantly-changing health-care environments. Excellent interpersonal, communication, and organizational skills.

EDUCATION

University of Colorado at Denver, Denver, Colorado
Master of Science in Nursing, Dean's Award for Excellence in Graduate Studies, Sigma Theta Tau International Sorority, Kappa Chapter, May 1999

Temple University, Philadelphia, Pennsylvania
Bachelor of Science in Nursing, 1993

CLINICAL AFFILIATIONS

North Street Internal Medicine, Denver, Colorado

- Completed 300-hour internship at HMO specializing in internal medicine. Performed physicals and well-women exams. Diagnosed and managed chronic and acute illnesses focusing on hypertension, diabetes, upper respiratory infections, and musculoskeletal injuries.

- Ordered and interpreted laboratory tests, requested radiological studies, prescribed appropriate medications; provided patient education and follow-up information highlighting disease prevention and referred patients when necessary.

- Utilized computerized health-care system to document patient information, arrange consults, and obtain laboratory findings.

West End Internal Medicine, Denver, Colorado

- Completed 90-hour internship with a private internal medicine practice. Administered a full range of nurse practitioner responsibilities for a diverse patient population with an emphasis on geriatric care.

- Specialized in patient prevention and treatment of hypertension, diabetes, and asthma.

University of Colorado at Denver Student Health Center, Denver, Colorado

- Completed 150-hour internship at an on-site student clinic. Diagnosed and treated patients with episodic illnesses including upper respiratory infections, sexually transmitted diseases, musculoskeletal injuries, and urinary tract infections.

- Provided patient education and a full range of support services.

NURSING EXPERIENCE

Greater Denver Medical Center, Denver, Colorado
Clinical Nurse, 1993 - present

- Administer care to cardiac patients recovering from coronary bypass surgery on a 22-to 30-bed unit. Execute charge nurse responsibilities.

- Perform telemetry interpretation, manage vasoactive drips and invasive lines, and conduct patient education.

- Initial two-year assignment with an 18-bed cardiovascular surgery and transplant unit and a 4-bed concentrated care unit.

Care Manager, 1996 - 1997

- Member of management team and resource/preceptor for a cardiac/surgical concentrated care unit.

- Performed staff evaluations and delivered annual education for staff training.

- Returned to clinical nursing responsibilities while pursuing full-time graduate studies.

CERTIFICATIONS/LICENSES

Adult Nurse Practitioner, American Nurses Credentialing Center (ANCC)

Registered Nurse (RN), Colorado

PROFESSIONAL AFFILIATIONS

American Academy of Nurse Practitioners

American Nurses Association

Alpha Kappa Alpha Sorority, Inc.

Former Vice President, Graduate Nursing School Olivian Society

DANIEL K. AVRAM, M.D.

Curriculum Vitae

6443 Lucket Lane
Brier, Washington 98036
(206) XXX-XXXX

EDUCATION

UNITED STATES INTERNATIONAL UNIVERSITY, Nairobi, Kenya
Graduate course in Family Therapy, September - December 1994

UNIVERSITY OF CALIFORNIA, Song Brown Fellowship Program, Modesto, California
Family Practice Fellow, 1988 - 1989

MODESTO GENERAL HOSPITAL, Modesto, California
Family Practice Residency, 1985 - 1988

UNIVERSITY OF WASHINGTON SCHOOL OF MEDICINE, Seattle, Washington
Doctor of Medicine (M.D.), 1984

WHITMAN COLLEGE, Walla Walla, Washington
Bachelor of Arts, Biology, 1979

WORK HISTORY

FAMILY PRACTICE

Brier Family Practice, 1995 - present
Partner in large, single-specialty family practice corporation in the northern Seattle area.

Locum Tenens in Family Medicine, 1991 - 1994
Locum work with five private family medicine practices in California and Washington states, and one private practice in Nairobi, Kenya.

John Lynam, M.D., Inc., 1988 - 1990
Private medical practice in Patterson, California, a predominantly Mexican and Mexican-American rural community.

Modesto General Hospital, 1988 - 1990
Private medical practice in Modesto, California.

Tabasco State Rural Health Program, 1984 - 1985
Physician in traveling village health clinic in Villahermosa, Mexico.

EMERGENCY MEDICINE

Locum Tenens in Emergency Medicine, 1992 - 1994
Emergency-room physician at County Trauma Center, Modesto General Hospital, Modesto, California and Del Puerto Hospital, Patterson, California.

Emergency Care, 1992 - 1995
Physician on call for tourist and film groups visiting remote areas of East Africa.

Nairobi Hospital, 1991 - 1992
Emergency-room physician, Nairobi, Kenya.

Manteca Hospital, 1988 - 1990
Emergency-room physician, Manteca, California.

RESEARCH

African Medical Research and Education Foundation (AMREF), Nairobi, Kenya
Consultant, 1995

Developed questionnaire for study on malaria treatment and outcome at Nairobi Hospital.

Aga Khan Hospital, Nairobi, Kenya
Departmental Evaluator, 1992

Evaluated flow patterns and frequency of diagnosis of emergency-room facilities.

Area Health Education Center, State of California
Principal Investigator, 1988 - 1990

Evaluated nutrition knowledge and training of family physicians in California.

Modesto General Hospital, Modesto, California
Member of Steering Committee for Medical Research, 1989 - 1990

TEACHING AND CURRICULUM DEVELOPMENT

Davis Free Community Clinic, Davis, California
Preceptor of medical students, 1995 - 1997

University of California, Davis, Davis, California
Assistant Clinical Professor, School of Medicine, Department of Family Practice, 1995 - 1997

Supervised and taught clinical skills to medical students and family practice residents during family practice clinical rotations.

African Medical Research and Education Foundation (AMREF), Nairobi, Kenya
Consultant, 1992 - 1995

Designed curriculum, taught clinical skills, and provided field supervision for community health-care workers and planners from East Africa.

Modesto General Hospital, Modesto, California
Preceptor, 1988 - 1990

Primary clinical supervisor for physician assistant program and teaching of family practice medical residents.

Area Health Education Center, Modesto, California
Research Fellow, 1988 - 1990

Developed nutrition curriculum for California residency programs in family medicine. Clinical training of residents at Modesto General Hospital. Didactic and clinical training of physician assistants and nurse practitioners.

HONORS AND AWARDS

Song-Brown Commission Fellowship, State of California, 1988 - 1989
Diplomate, American Academy of Family Physicians, 1988 - 1995; Re-certified, 1995 - 2001
Chief Resident, Modesto General Hospital, Modesto, California, 1987 - 1988

PROFESSIONAL AFFILIATIONS

American Academy of Family Practice, 1986 - present

United Health Medical Group, Inc. (Independent Physician Association for Davis Area), Member, Board of Directors, 1996 - 1997

Sutter-Davis Hospital, Davis, California, Member, Active Staff, 1995 - present

Woodland Memorial Hospital, Woodland, California, Member, Courtesy Staff, 1995 - present

Kenya Medical Association, 1991 - 1994

American Medical Association, 1983 - 1990

California Coastal Research Groups, 1988 - 1990

Stanislaus County Child and Infant Care Association, Inc., Member, Board of Directors, 1988 - 1990

National Coalition Against Health Fraud, 1988 - 1990

LANGUAGES

English, native; Spanish, fluent; Swahili, conversational.

SELECTED PAPERS AND PUBLICATIONS

"Hidden Agendas in Patient Care."
Invited lecture presented to the University of Davis Pre-Medical Society, Davis, California, May 1999.

"Retrospective Review of Emergency Room Patient Flow Patterns and Frequency of Diagnosis."
Analysis and recommendations for the Aga Khan Hospital, Nairobi, Kenya, June 1992.

Avram, D.K., Gossel, C., Welsher, J.
"Nutrition Education for Family Practice Residents," *Journal of Family Medicine*, 1:837-839, 1990.

"Teaching and Learning Outpatient Nutrition."
Teaching Seminar presented at the Society of Teachers of Family Medicine Annual Meeting, Nashville, Tennessee, May 1990.

"The State of Nutrition Knowledge Among Physicians."
Paper presented to the California Area Health Education Center, Statewide Program Advisory Committee Meeting and Annual Conference, Sacramento, May 1989.

"Feeding Patients Nutritional Advice: Tasting What We Dish Out."
Paper presented at University of California, Davis, Family Practice Residency Network Conference, Yosemite, California, March 1989.

"The Barefoot Doctors of Mexico's Oil Boom."
Paper presented to the University of California, Davis, Family Practice Residency Network Conference, March 1986.

"Delivery of Health Care in Craig, Alaska."
Paper presented to the University of Washington, Department of Family Practice, September 1983.

WAYNE WRIGHT
88 Second Avenue
New York, New York 10002
(212) XXX-XXXX

QUALIFICATIONS SUMMARY

Sixteen years' experience in writing, editing, and hands-on publication management.

- Effectively develop and coordinate projects from budgeting, copy editing, and generating stories to project oversight, design, and layout.
- Work closely with writers to successfully improve copy and translate complex ideas into understandable prose.

WORK HISTORY

Print Media

- Associate Editor of newsletter, *Inside the Market*, with circulation of 20,000, and stock report, *Stocks: Hot Picks*, Market Publishers Inc. 1996 - present.
- Associate Editor of newsletter, *Business Home Base*, with circulation of 12,000, New Business Publications. 1994 - 1996.
- Founding Editor and Partner of *Memphis Business Report*, a monthly tabloid with circulation of 15,000. Directed editorial and production for more than 1,500 pages a year. Handled concurrent responsibilities of Editor-in-Chief, Managing Editor, Copy Editor, and Production Manager. Supervised a staff of seven. 1988 - 1994.
- *Memphis Business Report* received 16 national awards for editorial and graphic excellence during leadership tenure.
- Received two national writing awards, *Memphis Business Report*.
- City Editor and Reporter, *Memphis Enterprise*, a community weekly with circulation of 40,000. 1980 - 1988.
- Reporter, *City City*, alternative weekly in Memphis with circulation of 10,000. 1979.

Radio and Television

- Numerous appearances on Tennessee Public Broadcasting. 1996 - 1999.
- Host, "Business Edition," cable public-access channel, 30-minute live call-in program. 1997.
- Monthly guest, "Economy Issues," WDDS-AM radio, 15-minute talk show. 1994 - 1995.
- Commentator, "Business Issues," WSSX-FM, twice-weekly 90-second business commentary, morning and evening drive times. 1990 - 1994.
- Frequent guest on TV talk shows concerning the economy. 1988 - 1989.

RELEVANT SKILLS

Public Speaking

- Frequent speaker to civic groups in Memphis area on economic outlook and business trends.

- Recurrent guest lecturer, Memphis University journalism classes, on business and feature writing.

Teaching

- Conducted seminar on "Trends in Business Writing" at Association of Southern Newspaper Publishers Association conference in Memphis, Tennessee, January 1989.

- Taught "Magazine Editing and Writing," short courses, and conference programs at University of Tennessee, Memphis, Tennessee.

- Taught "Principles of Magazine Editing" at Tennessee State University, Nashville, Tennessee.

EDUCATION

Bachelor of Arts, Journalism, 1979
Tennessee State University, Nashville, Tennessee

PROFESSIONAL AFFILIATIONS

Memphis Press Club

JULIA MARTINELLI
81 Wildwood Way
Philadelphia, Pennsylvania 19140
(215) XXX-XXXX

CAREER SUMMARY

Real-estate professional with top-notch performance. Extensive experience spanning general brokerage to new home, condominium, land, and investment sales. Solid financing background.

- Recognized specialist and top producer in home sales and closings in recessionary markets, project start-ups, and close-outs.
- Exceptional negotiator, achieving top dollar for seller/builder.
- Outstanding interpersonal skills, effectively communicating with individuals at all organizational levels.

EXPERIENCE

Small & Miller Realtors, Philadelphia, Pennsylvania
Community Sales Manager, New Home Sales, 1996 - 2001

- Successfully marketed and sold townhouses and single-family homes ranging from $130,000 to $769,000. Chosen to generate and close sales in projects with outstanding inventory or slow-moving properties.

Sales Performance

- Sold five townhouses following a Small & Miller auction in Philadelphia, Pennsylvania, at prices $40,000 to $50,000 higher than the auction prices.
- Sold and settled 44 homes in Meadow Park, a Turner Homes project located in Bucks County, significantly surpassing prior year sales of only six.
- Sold three luxury custom homes within three and a half months in Darby, Pennsylvania, during a market downturn and on a project that sold only one custom home in the prior eight months.
- Assumed sales responsibility in an upscale Darby community and sold six homes in 12 weeks during a recessionary period, exceeding prior seven months' record of only five sales.

Barker Corporation, Philadelphia, Pennsylvania
Community Sales Manager, New Home Sales, 1988 - 1996

- Achieved top performance selling new residential homes ranging from $250,000 to $800,000.
- Managed full sales life cycle from qualifying clients, demonstrating products, designing house plans, locating financing options, negotiating pricing and contracts, and closing sales to settlement.
- Wrote advertisements and developed strategic marketing plans for diverse projects.
- Selected to sell luxury homes in a gated golf course community in King of Prussia. Quickly sold villas and single-family homes for top dollar despite prior real-estate auction.

Steven Lawrence, Esquire, Harrisburg, Pennsylvania
Sales and Administration, 1986 - 1991

- Collaborated with attorney to manage personal real-estate investments. Simultaneously worked with Timmer Corporation and sold the last five houses in only five weeks in a hard-to-sell project.

Timmer Corporation, Harrisburg, Pennsylvania
New Home Sales, 1982 - 1985

- Broke sales records by selling 33 homes within initial eight months of employment.

National Financial Services (a Magna-owned company), Newark, New Jersey
Condominium Sales Associate, 1981 - 1982

- Marketed and sold condominium and residential recreational facilities.

Cooks Realtors, Wilmington, Delaware
Real Estate Salesperson, 1980 - 1981

- Sold 58 condominiums under the Condominium Sales Division in one quarter. Earned "Top Salesman of the Quarter Award."

Powers Corporation, Wilmington, Delaware
Real Estate Marketing and Sales Director, 1978 - 1980

- Established the sales organization of a newly formed company in the home building industry. Managed all aspects of sales and marketing including loan applications, advertising, and settlements.

Small & Miller Realtors, Chester, Pennsylvania
Real Estate Salesperson, 1976 - 1977

- Recognized for exceeding all sales performance during initial three weeks of tenure, selling and closing nine homes within three weeks of the Christmas holiday.

Griffin Communities Corp., Chester, Pennsylvania
Real Estate Salesperson, 1975 - 1976

EDUCATION

Attend ongoing continuing education classes in real estate at N.I.R.E.

University of Pennsylvania, Philadelphia, Pennsylvania; completed extensive general course work and classes in business and all facets of real estate.

LICENSES

Licensed Realtor, Pennsylvania

MELANIE MINOR

76 First Avenue, Dallas, Texas 75246   (214) XXX-XXXX

SUMMARY OF QUALIFICATIONS

Results-oriented business professional with progressive experience and solid achievements in the retail industry. Enthusiastic team player, working effectively with management to meet corporate objectives. Careful and thorough planner, executing projects with discipline and undiverted attention to detail.

EXPERIENCE

NEIMAN MARCUS
Dallas, Texas, 1989 - present

Manager, Collectors Department, 1997 - present

♦ Direct operations for high-end women's designer fashions at a flagship specialty department store. Department ranks #1 in regional volume with $2 million in annual sales.

♦ Build, train, and manage a productive selling staff and utilize technology and systems to maximize operations. Recruit, hire, train, schedule, counsel, and evaluate staff performance.

♦ Motivate sales team to promote business, increase volume, develop clientele, and enhance productivity for design collections including Giorgio Armani Le Collezioni, Donna Karan Collection, Calvin Klein, ESCADA, Dolce & Gabbana, Antonio Fusco, Lanvin, Victor Alfaro, and Helmut Lang.

♦ Point of contact among buyers, store management, and sales associates to enhance product knowledge and ensure delivery of exceptional customer service to meet high corporate standards and customer expectations.

♦ Select, coach, and cultivate potential managers. Provide strategies to facilitate goal achievement for top sales performers.

♦ Maintain accurate department records to reflect markdowns, price changes, vendor claims, and merchandise transfers.

Sales Associate, Collectors Department, 1996 - 1997

♦ Developed and expanded clientele in a commissioned sales environment, consistently providing superior customer service.

Sales Associate, Savvy Department, 1990 - 1996

♦ Established a personal clientele in the fashion-forward, cutting-edge women's sportswear department.

♦ Recognized with the "All Star" award, the highest honor given to sales associates for productivity, team spirit, and delivering outstanding customer service.

Sales Associate, Kidswear Girls, 1989 - 1990

♦ Participated in grand opening and sold merchandise at newly opened branch store.

EDUCATION

Texas A&M University, College Station, Texas, Bachelor of Arts in Elementary Education, 1985

HARRIS BLOCK
101 Monroe Avenue, Rochester, New York 14600
Work (716) XXX-XXXX   Home (716) XXX-XXXX   E-mail: Hblock@bbx.com

PROFESSIONAL PROFILE

Senior executive with solid achievements in managing finance operations in the public sector. Consensus builder and dynamic leader, motivating staff to exceed county-wide priorities. Effective communicator with excellent interpersonal skills and demonstrated ability in building collaborative relationships.

SIGNIFICANT ACHIEVEMENTS

- Represented a diverse, complex, urban government by effectively working with elected officials, senior managers, citizens, public-interest groups, and the media at all organizational levels in local, state, and federal jurisdictions.

- Led the Monroe County Department of Management and Finance through the budget-adoption process for FY 2000 with a $620-million operating budget and $505-million Capital Improvement Program during senior-management transition.

- Successfully directed the presentation to preserve Monroe's AAA/Aaa bond rating and coordinated the sale of $80 million of bonds at a very favorable 5% interest rate.

- Spearheaded and coordinated the first county-wide effort to establish a Technology Strategic Plan, resulting in increased funds and significant technology improvements.

- Negotiated and resolved tax issues with a Fortune 500 company headquartered in Rochester and created an incentive package for them to both remain and expand.

- Actively participated in the County Manager's Executive Leadership team, 1994, 1995, 1999.

WORK HISTORY

MONROE COUNTY, Rochester, New York, 1983 - present

Acting Director Department of Management and Finance, 1999 - present

- Selected to direct finance, budget, tax policy, accounting, audit, purchasing, and real estate operations for a full-service urban county government with an annual budget of $620 million.

- Manage a staff of 55 that prepares and monitors capital and operating budgets, manages debt, forecasts revenue, evaluates programs, audits compliance, assesses property, purchases goods and services, and ensures fiscal accountability for county funds.

- Launched reengineering initiatives, creating a high-performance organization that improves department morale and productivity. Appointed employee task forces to restructure and redesign work processes, institute stress-reduction programs, and enhance internal communications.

- Appointed by County Manager as Retirement Board Trustee of a $1-billion fund.

Senior Tax Policy Coordinator, 1995 - 1999

- Identified, mediated, and resolved complex and controversial business tax issues by teaming with the Commissioner of the Revenue, Treasurer, County Attorney, Department of Economic Development, and business interest groups.

- Researched issues and lobbied the State legislature, municipal associations, and regional jurisdictions to establish responsible tax policy.

Acting Director of Libraries, 1994 - 1995

- Directed seven-branch county-wide library system with 180 employees and $8.3-million operating budget. Instrumental in attaining a major public Internet technology grant for the libraries and implementing a LAN CD-ROM public information center.

Administrative Services Division Chief, 1988 - 1995

- Administered personnel, finance, and facilities functions for the county-wide library system. Oversaw capital and operating funds and federal, state, and private grants. Supported a department-wide fund-raising effort with the community, raising over $100,000 for enhancements to newly renovated and expanded central library.

- Nominated by County Manager and completed the Management Excellence Program at the Weldon Cooper Center for Public Service, University of Rochester, May 1991.

- Selected in 1990 as one of six county Certified Management Trainers to train county managers.

- Chosen as one of ten employees for a year-long senior management mentoring program in 1989.

Assistant to the Director, 1988

- Assigned to Department of Community, Planning, Housing and Development to assist in reorganizing processes and functions. Prepared budget in coordination with division chiefs and program managers.

Senior Metro Analyst, 1983 - 1988

- Staff liaison to the Rochester Metropolitan Area Transportation Authority. Lobbied and negotiated for metro issues impacting the county and briefed Monroe County Board representative.

- Selected to head up special projects including health plan evaluations and federal aid cuts.

- Presented "Monroe County Exceptional Employee Award" in 1988.

FAIRFAX COUNTY, Fairfax, Virginia, 1980 - 1983

Senior Budget Analyst, Office of Management and Budget, 1980 - 1983

- Progressive promotions to manage $120 million in funds for the Department of Housing. Analyzed budget requests, recommended funding levels, and prepared the executive budget and financial plan.

- Monitored and forecasted expenditures including federal and state grants and recommended feasible reductions during periods of fiscal constraint.

EDUCATION

Georgetown University, Washington, D.C.
M.A. in Government and Politics, 1981; awarded graduate assistant full scholarship
B.A. in Public Administration, 1979; Dean's List; **Public Administration Certificate**, 1980

COMMUNITY/POLITICAL INVOLVEMENT

Geraldine Ferraro Campaigns for Congress and Vice Presidency, 1978, 1980, 1982, 1984
Board Member, Youth Leadership Metropolitan Rochester, Inc., 1998 - present; Meals on Wheels, 1995 - 1999

PROFESSIONAL AFFILIATIONS

Graduate, Leadership Rochester, Class of 1999
Government Finance Officers Association (GFOA)

CAROLINE J. SMILEY
7766 Canyon Drive, Campbell, California 95008
(408) XXX-XXXX   E-mail: CSmiley@vvv.com

PROFESSIONAL PROFILE

Creative and persuasive senior telecommunications manager, integrating information technology to achieve improvements in business process, network management, and revenue growth. Proven record in addressing customer and user needs with excellent interpersonal and oral/written communication skills. Expertise with the following technologies:

- Network Management Systems
- Fraud Management Systems
- Data Mining/Warehousing

- Service Activation/Provisioning
- Calling Card Platforms
- Systems Integration

EDUCATION

San Francisco State University, San Francisco, California
M.S., Information Systems Management, 1999; **B.S., Business Management**, 1980

EXPERIENCE

XYZ Solutions, Palo Alto, California, 1998-present
VICE PRESIDENT, MARKETING, 1998-present

Rapid promotions with a start-up network management solutions provider. Design and develop marketing programs and strategies for a suite of network management products and services for the domestic and international telecommunications industry.

Establish strategic partnerships with other network management solution providers to enhance product offerings and maximize potential revenue.

Launched the first structured marketing effort that has significantly contributed to rapid revenue growth.

Teleserve, San Jose, California, 1993-1997
SENIOR PROGRAM MANAGER, 1994-1997

Managed innovative technical programs for an international telecommunications provider.

Directed multiple teams designing, developing, and implementing projects including an enterprise-wide (2,500-user) corporate intranet, a client/server, Unix-based, Oracle/relational database management system that supported 500+ users located at 65 sites to manage Teleserve's fiber optic network. Led several prototyping initiatives that drove Teleserve's enterprise-wide data mining/warehousing strategy.

SENIOR PROJECT MANAGER, 1993-1994

Managed teams in planning, testing, and implementing a variety of software development projects. Reported to senior executive management team.

Directed a ten-member team in the reengineer of the customer billing process utilizing automated tools, process redesign, and system tuning techniques.

Reduced overall billing time by 30% and doubled the capability to process switched circuit billing records.

Stragicom, Inc., Palo Alto, California, 1987-1993
AREA MANAGER, SYSTEM SUPPORT GROUP, 1990-1993

Oversaw systems support for a large software developer specializing in network integration and open network management software development projects. Managed and developed support staff, business/information systems plans, network design, competitive benchmark planning, quality assurance testing, and support processes/procedures for a large computer installation including three East Coast locations (18 systems).

Redesigned process to consolidate multiple information system groups into one organization. Improved operating efficiencies and reduced overall costs by an estimated $450,000 over three years. Recognized with "Stragicom Excellence Award."

Collaborated with Stragicom's software development partners to migrate software development applications to Stragicom's platform.

Created process to leverage software support function and generate professional services revenue.

MANAGER, INFORMATION SYSTEMS, 1988-1990

Managed finance, contracts, operations, and technical publications staff. Planned and administered technology upgrades, Local Area Network (LAN) support, and resource allocations for a variety of operational environments with 250+ users.

Achieved cost reductions and implemented expense controls through introduction of new solutions and improved operating efficiencies.

"Regional Team Award" for excellence in system operations and management.

SENIOR BUSINESS ANALYST, 1987-1988

Enhanced organizational effectiveness and productivity by developing and implementing processes that utilized emerging technology.

National Telecommunications Society, San Francisco, California, 1980-1987
MANAGER, DATA PROCESSING APPLICATIONS, 1986-1987
SYSTEMS ANALYST, 1983-1986
INTERNAL AUDITOR, 1980-1983

Managed technical business application programs for a two-million-member association with 100 clubs. Recommended conversion to senior executives of leading-edge programs for financial, retail, insurance agency, and travel agency applications.

Marketed application products to club management and designed new products/services to satisfy club needs.

Conducted full life-cycle development for software projects.

TRAINING

- Marketing Technology-Based Solutions
- Technical Account Management
- Structured Methodologies and Design
- Strategic Planning for Information Systems
- System Quality and Productivity
- LAN Concepts and Topologies

- Information Engineering
- Consulting for Added Value
- Engineering Economics/Financial Analysis
- TCP/IP LAN Concepts
- System Architect (CASE Tool)
- Logical Database Design

Preparing Scannable Résumés

2

Self-Test Your Savvy in Preparing Scannable Résumés: Will Your Résumé Survive the Scanner?

The following self-test is a tool to help you assess your readiness in writing and producing a scannable résumé. The objective is not to get the highest score possible, but to pinpoint areas that you can strengthen to produce a scannable résumé that will position you as one of the top-ranked applicants.

1. I can use my traditional résumé when submitting a résumé that will be scanned by a computer. — T/F __
2. I need to choose a fixed-width font for my scannable résumé. — T/F __
3. Scannable résumés should be one to two pages. — T/F __
4. I must customize a scannable résumé for each position I'm pursuing. — T/F __
5. I should use plenty of key words in my scannable résumé. — T/F __
6. The more often I use the same key words, the better. — T/F __
7. Scannable résumés are often kept in employer databases for six months. — T/F __
8. I should research job requirements when preparing a scannable résumé. — T/F __
9. I can detail more experience on my scannable résumé. — T/F __
10. My experience and skills speak for themselves. — T/F __
11. Scannable résumés should not have bullets. — T/F __

12. I should avoid acronyms and jargon on my scannable résumé. T/F __
13. Scannable résumés are used mostly for high-tech jobs. T/F __
14. It is imperative that I follow application requirements when preparing my scannable résumé. T/F __
15. I should start my scannable résumé from scratch. T/F __
16. Résumé-scanning systems read text and graphics. T/F __
17. If I have professional training in a specific area but no practical experience, the training may count towards meeting job qualifications. T/F __
18 White, beige, and grey colored papers are best for scannable résumés. T/F __
19. It's okay to use ruling lines in my scannable résumé. T/F __
20. I shouldn't fold my scannable résumé. T/F __
21. Scannable résumés should be tailored for each job. T/F __
22. Italics don't scan well but uppercase scans fine. T/F __
23. I'll avoid using bold even though some organizations allow you to use it. T/F __
24. I should include my name and page number on each succeeding page of my scannable résumé. T/F __
25. I should not staple my pages together. T/F __
26. When conducting my search, I should specifically inquire whether organizations require scannable résumés. T/F __
27. Times New Roman is one of the best fonts to use in either 10 or 12 point. T/F __
28. I can't use underlining in a scannable résumé. T/F __
29. My scannable résumé should be in a chronological format. T/F __
30. Some employers allow you to send your scannable résumé by facsimile. T/F __

Total: _____

Score 1 point for each "True" response and 0 for each "False" response, EXCEPT for questions 1, 3, 6, 10, 12, 13, 15, 16, 18, 19, 27. *For these questions only*, **subtract** 1 point for each "True" response. Record your total. A score below +17 indicates that you would benefit from practicing the scannable résumé-writing techniques discussed in this chapter. (*Note:* It is possible to have a negative score.)

Scannable Résumé Fundamentals

The downsizing trend began in the early 1990s when *Fortune* 500 companies announced massive layoffs. By the end of the decade, it was hard to find an employee who hadn't been affected. The downsizing trend continues on both a small- and large-scale basis as private and public sector organizations search for ways to reduce costs and achieve profitability.

The human resources function, a nonrevenue-producing area, was a primary target during downsizing. While organization headcounts declined during these transitions, the downsizing trend didn't reduce the number of résumés in circulation. Both public and private sector organizations searched for automated solutions to deal with résumé volumes and staffing needs. Electronic skills-assessment processing systems, also known as résumé-scanning systems, provided an immediate solution—a cost-effective in-house recruitment function with minimal staffing.

Résumés are first scanned into these computer systems as an image. Then Optical Character Recognition (OCR) software looks at the image to distinguish every character (letters and numbers) and creates an unformatted text file (also known as ASCII or American Standard Code for Information Interchanges). Artificial intelligence (AI) or expert systems reads the text and extracts information including your name, address, phone number, skills, years of experience, and education.

Hiring managers establish position criteria for their job openings based on skills, experience, education, training, and credentialing requirements. The criteria are fed into the system and then a search is made for résumés that include those requirements or "key" words. The computer makes a "hit" each time it matches one of your credentials or skills to a requirement for which it is searching; the likelihood of your selection as a top candidate increases with each "hit."

Employers who use these systems are happy with the results. They've minimized staffing costs while efficiently handling, sorting, storing, and responding to increasing volumes of résumés. Large private and public sector organizations are the biggest users, but as technology costs decline and smaller organizations turn to outsourcing, you will find more and more organizations using résumé-scanning systems.

Tip: The more skills and information you provide in your scannable résumé, the more opportunities you'll have for your qualifications to match available positions.

When to Send a Scannable Résumé

Before you apply for a position, you must identify an organization's application requirements. You'll need a scannable résumé for:

1. Newspaper employment listings that request one.
2. Organizations whose Web sites state they scan résumés.
3. Job announcements that request you send a résumé that can be scanned.
4. Organizations that publish application requirements indicating they use résumé-scanning systems.

Tip: If you are particularly interested in working for an organization, check its Web site or call its human resources department to determine whether it scans résumés.

What to Say in Scannable Résumés

Scannable résumés are unique. They not only differ from traditional résumés in format and content, but because of the proliferation of different scanning hardware and software, each organization has its own requirements. Suggested basic guidelines include:

1. Carefully follow the instructions organizations provide in their newspaper employment listings, Web sites, and printed application requirements that detail how they want you to write and prepare scannable résumés.

2. Use a marker to highlight key job requirements, qualifications, and buzz words used in the job announcement or advertisement.

3. Mention all of your experience, skills, abilities, education, training, professional licenses, certifications, publications, and affiliations that qualify you for the position.

4. Match your qualifications to the requirements you've highlighted. For example, let's say you are a female and own your own business. If the announcement states you will be conducting training programs for women-owned businesses, introduce that particular work experience with "Established and managed a women-owned business." This added description increases your chances of a "hit" or "key" word match.

5. Evaluate every job you have had, paid or volunteer, that meets the desired criteria. There may be experiences in your past that you no longer include in your résumé that bolster your credentials.

6. Generously use "key" words: technical, skill, or industry terms used frequently in your occupation or industry.

7. Bolster your credentials with acronyms and jargon specific to your industry; human eyes will also read these résumés so spell out the acronyms for those readers.

in Scannable Résumés

1. No matter how much you want the job, don't play to the scanner, including qualifications that don't exist. You'll have to interview for the job and any discrepancies will be detected.

2. Avoid repeating the same "key" words again and again. Instead, try using statements and synonyms that increase your chances of another match. For example, use "bilingual in Spanish and English" in your summary and state "fluent in Spanish and English" under a skills section.

3. Don't state experience in general terms such as "completed organization-wide audit projects." Enhance the statement with key words:

"completed compliance, fraud, performance, operational, and financial audit projects."

4. Don't assume that a computer knows the different elements that make up your responsibilities. You might state "market, plan, and execute small to large meetings and events for a full-service hotel." Don't stop there; you'll increase your chances of matching key words by adding the sentence "Work with association, individual, government, and corporate clients in the telecommunications, health care, and banking industries to arrange annual conferences, board meetings, social events, seminars, and retreats for 2 to 2,000 attendees."

5. Don't place your emphasis on action verbs only; balance your text with nouns, verbs, adjectives, and adverbs to maximize "key" word hits.

 ## in Scannable Résumés

You'll use a scannable résumé when applying for a specific job opportunity you've identified through a job announcement, newspaper employment listing, employment listing on a Web site, or through a referral.

- STEP 1: Discover as much as you can about the position to determine the desired and preferred qualifications.

- STEP 2: If you have a documented announcement, read it carefully and underscore the key requirements or "key" words.

- STEP 3: If you are unable to locate the job requirements, put on your detective cap and do some sleuthing. Make up your own list by reviewing the newspaper employment listings for jobs like the one you are applying for, requesting job descriptions and announcements from your network, and accessing Web sites of different organizations to evaluate their job descriptions and announcements.

- STEP 4: Save your traditional résumé as a new document and begin to further describe and expand on your experiences, accomplishments, education, training, and credentials.

- STEP 5: Keep a list of the job requirements you've detailed and use as many of the "key" words as you can in your descriptions.

- STEP 6: Address every requirement that you can even if it is at an elementary rather than experienced level.

- STEP 7: Continue to document and enhance your credentials until you are satisfied you have addressed every possible requirement.

- STEP 8: Create a strong summary that details how you qualify for the position, highlighting your experience, skills, expertise, strengths, and abilities.

Tip: If there is a qualification you are missing and you have time, register for a course in that topic and then include on your résumé that you are either registered or attending ** course with anticipated completion date of **.

Words to Use in Scannable Résumés

Résumé-scanning systems will be set to search for words and phrases that are essential to a specific job responsibility. Many of these words will be nouns but that doesn't mean you should abandon active and accomplishment-oriented verbs; rather, include them all. Because each résumé is unique to the required job responsibilities, you will have to cull a list of words that are integral to your targeted position. Here are the types of words you should consider.

JOB TITLES

accountant	corrections officer
actuary	director
adjuster	economist
administrator	engineer
aircraft pilot	financial manager
architect	insurance broker
auditor	landscape architect
bank manager	librarian
bookkeeper	manager
chef	producer
computer engineer	publicist
controller	trainer
cook	treasurer
counselor	

Elaborate on the titles, such as: Sales or account associate, representative, executive, or manager.

Job titles can vary so you may want to include all applicable job title variations in your résumé. For example:

accountant, auditor, controller

administrative assistant, executive assistant, word processor, legal secretary

administrator, billing manager, customer service manager, credit and
   collections manager

attorney and lawyer

buyer and purchasing agent

instructor and professor

nurse, registered nurse, and staff nurse

personnel manager, human resources manager, organizational development specialist, employee relations manager, HR generalist, benefits and compensation manager

physician and doctor

police officer and law enforcement professional

public relations specialist, publicist, media relations manager, and press officer

recruiter, staffing coordinator, and employment interviewer

restaurant and food service manager

trainer, speaker, and lecturer

writer, editor, and author

SKILL AREAS

Any particular skill areas that are pertinent to your occupation should be included, for example:

- accounting could be accounts payable, accounts receivable, payroll, tax preparation, or tax filing
- computers would generate details on languages, operating systems, software, or hardware
- language fluency at your skill level, for example: knowledge of, conversant, fluent, or proficient in Spanish, French, Italian, or German

SPECIALIZED AREAS THAT DESCRIBE YOUR FOCUS

- convention planning
- cost accounting
- corporate promotions
- geriatric nursing
- governmental accounting

NOUNS

- counseling
- speaking
- training
- writing

CERTIFICATIONS

Designations should be stated after your name and spelled out in a Certifications or Licenses section:

CIA	CPA	MD
CISA	LPN	Ph.D.
CMA	LSW	RN

Key Words for 16 Occupations

ACCOUNTING

accounts payable

accounts receivable

accruals

annual

audit

balance sheet

bank reconciliations

budget

cash flow

controls

corporation

cost accounting

cost control

cost-saving

credits

debits

depreciation

expense

federal tax

financial statements

generally accepted auditing standards (GAAS)

generally accepted accounting principles (GAAP)

general ledger

government accounting

income statement

income tax

individual

ledger

management accounting

management letters

monthly

partnerships

payroll

planning

public accounting

quarterly

reports

sales tax

solutions

state tax

summary

trial balances

ADMINISTRATIVE

appointments

calendar

confidential

contracts

correspondence

database

efficiency

expense

files

forms

general office duties

hardware

meetings

office duties

procedures

production

productivity

proposals

proofreading

relationships

reports

software

spreadsheet

statistical

tables

technical

transcription

travel

type

word processing

AUDITING

audits

audit testing

certified

compliance

controls

exit conference

financial

findings

fraud

generally accepted
    auditing standards
    (GAAS)

generally accepted
    accounting principles
    (GAAP)

internal audit

internal controls

management
    procedures

mismanagement

operational

program

records

reports

waste

BANKING

accounts

applications

bank operations

bank services

branch

cash drawer

certificates of deposit
  (CDs)

checking

commercial

commercial bank

consumer

credit applications

escrow

estate

expenses

income

investments

loans

merger

mortgages

notes

post-closing

safe deposit boxes

savings and loan

savings bank

tellers cash

trust

COMMUNICATIONS

advertising

broadcast

cablecast

campaign

circulation

direct mail

editorial

magazine

media

media events

news releases

newsletter

newspaper

press releases

printed

production

reporting

scripts

video

COMPUTER/TECHNICAL

applications
based
business development
CASE tools
changes
client
client-server
circuit
COBOL
concept
conversion
data
database
delivery
design
disk
documentation
end-user
files
functional
global
GUI
hardware
implementation
information technology
   (IT)

installation
Internet
Internetworking
Java
life cycle
local area network
   (LAN)
maintenance
management
   information systems
   (MIS)
Microsoft Certified
   Systems Engineer
   (MCSE)
modifications
network
online
performance
peripherals
PCs
plans
printers
program management
programs
project
relational database

reports
risk
scripts
software
SQL
system design
system performance
system requirements
technologies
test
tools
topologies
troubleshoot
wide area network
   (WAN)
Windows
tape drive
technical specifications
terminals
upgrade
VSAM
workstations
UNIX
user manuals
voice

EDUCATION

alternative

at-risk

cognitive thinking

conduct disorders

curriculum

developmental levels

developmentally
   appropriate

gifted

gifted and talented

hands-on

high-risk

inclusion classroom

inclusive

individual educational
   plan (IEP)

individualized

instructional styles

interdisciplinary

language arts

language expression

learning disabilities
   (LD)

lesson plans

mainstream

multicultural

parent–teacher

performance-based

process writing

school-wide

special needs

styles of learning

teaching methodologies

thematic

transition plans (TP)

whole language

FINANCE

accounting

accounts

actual

annual

balance sheets

budgets

capital

cash flow

cash management

cash manager

cash receipts

chief operating officer
   (COO)

controller

controllership

costs

cost accounting

credit

credit manager

current

earnings

financial instruments

financial reporting

financial statements

forecast

general ledger

income statements

instruments

investors

outlook

overhead

operations

procedures

regulations

regulatory

reports

requirements

risk

sales

stock holders

transactions

treasurer

HOSPITALITY

administration	flagship	property
ballroom	food and beverage	quality
banquet	full-service	reservation
board meetings	guest	restaurant
budget	hotel	retreats
catering	locations	room
charity	logistics	sales
conference	luxury	seminars
contracts	meeting space	sites
convention	menus	social events
costs	occupancy	upscale
events	on-site	volunteers
fine dining	operations	wait staff

HUMAN RESOURCES

affirmative action	job descriptions	procedures
benefits	manuals	programs
career development	medical	recruitment
compensation	orientation	retention
dental	outplacement	screening
discipline	payroll	staffing
employee benefits	performance standards	training
401(k)	pre-employment	tuition reimbursement
handbooks	testing	workshops
job analysis		

LAW

appellate	documents	personal injury
attorney	employment law	practice
bankruptcy	estate	pre-litigation
breach	evidence	product liability
cases	factual	second chair
complaints	files	settlement
confidential	legal	sole practitioner
contract	jury	specialty
court	lawyer	taxes
criminal	lead counsel	torte
defense	liability	trademark
discovery	litigation	trial
disputes	mediator	trust
docket	paralegal	Westlaw
documentary	patent	

LAW ENFORCEMENT/SECURITY

antitrust	crime scene	physical evidence
arrest	disputes	police officer
bank fraud	embezzlement	response
bribery	evidence	report writing
cases	identification	safety
conflict of interest	incidents	security
confrontations	informant	sensitive
convictions	investigation	squad
counterintelligence	latent prints	surveillance
criminal	patrol	white-collar crime
crime	physical	

MANAGEMENT/SENIOR EXECUTIVE

acquisition	management	pre-merger
budget	markets	profit and loss (P&L)
business	matrix management	profitable
cross-functional	mergers	profitability
diverse	multilocation	promotions
domestic	multimillion	revenue
executive	operation	stability
fiscal	organizational	successful
global	organization-wide	team
goals	overall	ventures
improvement	plan	worldwide
international		

RETAIL

assortment	inventory	ready-to-wear
branch	location	relationships
chain	loss	resources
clientele	markdown	retail
concept	mark-up	revenue
discount	merchandise	sales
displays	merchandise manager	shortage
divisions	merchandising	shrinkage
divisional manager	operations	special events
financial	openings	start-up
goals	performance	store manager
grand opening	private label	stores
gross margin	productivity	strategic
growth	profitability	upscale
high-volume	profits	vendor
in-store	promotional	

SALES/MARKETING

account executive	expectations	promote
account management	full service	qualifying
accounts	goal	quota
benefits	leads	rank
business development	loyalty	recognition
canvassing	market	regional
client	market share	relationships
client base	national	retention
clientele	new	revenue
closing	niche	sales
cold calls	objective	sales representative
commission	penetrating	services
competitive	performance	strategies
consistent	performer	target
contract	potential	territory
customer	products	top
customer base	profit	vertical marketing
existing		

TRAVEL AND TOURISM

Apollo	hotel	ticketing
agency	international	timeshare
airline	package	tourists
bookings	railway	tours
cruise	rental	travel
destination	reservations	vacation
domestic	Sabre	visitors
global		

Phrases to Use in Scannable Résumés

Hiring managers often have the capability of setting the criteria for their searches so you can never feel secure in knowing exactly what "key" words the computer will be seeking. It is in your best interest to fortify your résumé with as many phrases and variations that demonstrate your capabilities. For example:

administer nursing process

award-winning advertising manager

client-server databases

collaborate with editorial, circulation, and marketing departments

comprehensive knowledge of pharmaceutical-related government rules and regulations

direct product development and customer service

employee benefits administration

establish retention marketing strategies

frequent speaker, writer, and trainer

IBM operating systems

knowledge of Microsoft Office 2000

maximize corporate profits

negotiate GSA contracts

PC-based relational databases

proficient in Microsoft Excel, Word, Access, PowerPoint

recognized specialist in organizational development (OD)

sell end-user software training services

65-bed trauma and neurology unit

top producer in invoice revenue

Sentences to Use in Scannable Résumés

Analyzed, designed, implemented, and tested a prototype using Visual C++ and MFC technologies.

Compose and type correspondence, proposals, contracts, forms, charts, tables, and lists.

Control revenue and expenses for a 3,000-member professional society.

Create and maintain databases utilizing WordPerfect and Microsoft Excel word-processing and spreadsheet programs.

Designed and developed Unix-based applications in a client-server environment.

Developed a Web-based application to search for misposted payments using ASP, JavaScript, and COMET technologies.

Financial leader of a ten-member cross-functional regional team, covering Washington to Arizona, charged with achieving 2000 gross margin plan of $50 million.

Inspect and observe workers to ensure compliance with federal, state, and local regulations for liquor consumption.

Led the launch and installation of 20 data centers providing a full suite of Internet services.

Managed desktop and LAN-related sales to eight Fortune 200 companies.

Market, sell, design, and deliver audiovisual presentation services to corporate, government, and nonprofit clients in the Chicago metropolitan area.

Oversaw contract bids, proposals, and pricing strategies for domestic XYZ operations.

Perform financial analysis and cost control and lead productivity initiatives that drive operating areas to reduce costs.

Plan and execute meetings, conventions, and social events at a 4-star, luxury hotel property.

Proficient in Microsoft Word, Excel, Access, and Corel WordPerfect.

Provide pre-sales support, application design consultation, and project management of interactive voice data and video services implementation.

Serve as Charge Nurse and Unit Supervisor on neuro-orthopedic 25-bed unit.

Paragraphs to Use in Scannable Résumés

Achieved $5.2 million in computer paper and business forms sales to commercial accounts. Generated business through effective specification writing and workflow analysis. Penetrated territory by establishing new vendor sources to meet customer demand for more diversified product line.

Complete rooms division and accounting responsibility for a 600-room convention hotel with $19.5 million in annual sales and 410 employees. Formulate and execute annual budget, capital expenditure plan, sales, and profit projections. Oversee accounting, front office, housekeeping, concierge, bell staff, laundry, night audit, payroll, and purchasing staffs.

Consult with managers, supervisors, and human resources personnel to coach clients through employee relations, conflict resolution, risk management, and organizational change issues. Provide on-site critical incidence management.

Developed the Document Production System (DPS), a menu-driven assembly software product utilizing Microsoft Word macro language. DPS resulted in an 80% reduction in cycle time for clients through the standardization of information gathering.

Direct marketing, advertising, public relations, communications, and media relations for a 274-restaurant operation in San Francisco and surrounding suburban areas. Manage an $18-million annual budget.

Initiate and conduct market research, analyze data, and identify product needs. Recommend a product roadmap by collaborating with legal, credit policy, portfolio management, operations, and systems departments.

Oversee all food and supplies; establish par levels, purchase all products, and consistently meet food cost budget. Collaborate with chef to create specials, implement daily par levels for prepped food, and control quality of prepped items.

Participated in construction and unit testing of document locator application, a UNIX server module that accepts search request from client application and performs distributed queries across the network. Conducted the analysis, design, construction, and testing of the subsystem with nine applications.

Provided pediatric nursing care in critical care unit. Administered medications, maintained central line catheters and ventilators, and performed endo-tracheal suctioning, sterile dressing changes, IV set ups and priming, and insertion of foley catheters.

Supported senior executive of international trade association. Maintained calendar, scheduled and planned meetings, tracked time reporting, and ordered supplies. Prepared and typed correspondence, overheads, and reports using Microsoft Word, PowerPoint, and Excel.

Special Situations

You're interested in a job but have no idea what qualifications they're seeking. Call the organization's human resources department and ask for a copy of the job announcement or job description. If the organization has none, ask for the name of the hiring manager and call him or her to discuss the job specifications. If you still can't locate anything definitive within the organization, use your network to locate a similar job description for another organization.

You have a list of job requirements and you don't meet all of them. Apply for the job anyway and include and expand upon all of your qualifications that match the job requirements. Think carefully to identify and include any training, education, or experience in your background that has relevance in the areas you feel are lacking.

∾ *You are not sure whether you should mail, fax, or electronically mail your scannable résumé.* You will often find an organization's delivery preference in its job advertisements and announcements and you should follow these directions carefully. If you cannot find an organization's preference, call the human resources department or search for employment information on its Web site.

Tip: When faxing your résumé, set the fax mode on your facsimile machine or fax board to "fine mode" for the clearest and best-quality copy.

∾ *You have experience ten years back that meets the job requirements.* Scanning systems search for key words and required qualifications so include any prior experience that will qualify you for the position no matter how far back. Format your experience chronologically and fill in the gaps between your current experience and those that match the requirements.

∾ *The position you are seeking requires experience in one specific area that you don't have.* If you meet the majority of the qualifications, apply for the position anyway. The employer may not be able to find someone who has all of its desired qualifications.

∾ *You don't have certification or licensure yet within the state where you are applying.* Some states have reciprocity for certification and licensure, so if that is the case, just include your current information. If you meet credentialing requirements from another state, there is no reciprocity involved, and you either are applying or have applied in your new state, you can include:

Certification K-6, Commonwealth of Massachusetts; currently acquiring certification for the Commonwealth of Virginia

∾ *You don't own a computer.* Look through the telephone directory to locate print shops or copy centers that rent computers by the hour. Some library systems and state employment commissions allow job seekers and the public to use their computers. A friend, family member, or colleague may have a personal computer to lend.

Formatting Scannable Résumés

Your résumé must be formatted properly to scan well. Standardized criteria include:

- Reverse chronological format to detail your experience and education.
- Your name, complete mailing address, and phone numbers (home, work, and electronic mail) centered on the first page.
- Section headings centered and left justification for all other text.
- As many pages as you need to chronicle your qualifications, but check specifications as each organization is different and some do limit the number of pages.
- Your name and page number on each succeeding page.
- Follow carefully any specific requirements on the sequential order of information.
- If the organization includes specific categories—such as professional development activities, specialized training, presentations, publications, software proficiency, honors, or memberships—search through your work history (paid and volunteer) to locate any experiences that match the requirements for those categories.
- Certifications and licenses that are required or preferred. Check your actual documents to state accurately your credentials, including the issuing state or organization and expiration if applicable.

Tip: Publications can include unpublished theses or handbooks, workbooks, directories, manuals, newsletters, or procedural guidelines. Just state the title of the publication and the year it was completed.

Producing Scannable Résumés

- STEP 1: Save your traditional résumé as a new document.
- STEP 2: Remove all special effects and desktop publishing features such as ruling lines, bullets, columns, and underline.

- STEP 3: Remove italics, ampersands (&), percent signs (%); they don't scan well.
- STEP 4: If you have a slash (/), for example TCP/IP or USA Today/ Gannett Corporation, add a space between the text and slash so they don't touch (TCP / IP or USA Today / Gannett Corporation).
- STEP 5: Choose a fixed-width font or standard typeface such as Times New Roman, Arial, Palatino, Futura, Optima, and Courier, preferably with a font size of 12 point; 10 point or 14 point are sometimes acceptable.

Tip: Do not use Times New Roman in 10; it is difficult for both the computer and the human eye to read.

- STEP 6: Avoid boldface text; some systems do accept it but others don't, so it makes sense to just eliminate it.
- STEP 7: Make it easy for the computer to read your text by balancing your résumé with plenty of white space.
- STEP 8: Print originals or make clean photocopies on $8^{1}/_{2} \times 11$-inch quality bond paper in white, which scans best. Use plain paper without marbling, mottling, or textures.
- STEP 9: Print on one side only.
- STEP 10: Paper clip your pages together; don't staple the pages.
- STEP 11: Send your résumé unfolded in a 9×12-inch envelope.

Tip: Many resources suggest you use Helvetica as a fixed-width font. The font Arial is a form of Helvetica.

Sample Scannable Résumés

Here are three sample scannable résumés.

LAWRENCE B. RILEY
9044 Miller Heights Road
Oakton, Virginia 22124
Home (703) XXX-XXXX   Work (703) XXX-XXXX
E-mail: lbr@xyz.com

QUALIFICATIONS SUMMARY

Technical manager with extensive experience in performance and capacity management. Versatile technical skills, applicable to a wide range of technologies.

COMPUTER SKILLS

Hardware: IBM S / 370 and S / 390 series, HDS and Amdahl plug compatible systems, UNIX SVR4 compatible systems, Unisys 1100, 2200, 5000, Tandem VLX, Cyclone and Himalaya, IBM compatible PCs, Apple Macintosh.

Software: IBM JCL, TSO, ISPF, Clist, VM / CMS, SAS, MXG, MICS, SCERT, ProSim, Athene, Analytical Modeling, Simulation Modeling, Windows NT / 98 / 2000, Microsoft Office, COBOL, Visual Basic, HTML, FrontPage, graphics programs.

TECHNICAL SKILLS

Computer performance evaluation, performance engineering, computer simulation, workload forecasting, configuration management, system tuning, network performance analysis, system selection and migration, GUI application development, Internet Web design and development, graphic development.

MANAGEMENT SKILLS

Project management, product life cycle planning, project cost evaluation, management reporting, business system planning, Request for Proposal (RFP) preparation, proposal evaluation, migration planning, report writing, technical training.

EXPERIENCE

Director of Technical Services, Technicomm Inc., Dulles, Virginia, 1992 - present

Direct the development and enhancement of a suite of capacity planning and computer sizing products including IBM mainframe-, UNIX-, and PC-based components. Oversee the delivery of consulting, pre-sales / post-sales, presentations, and customer support to Fortune 500 companies and government agencies.

Define functional requirements and specifications; perform hands-on application development. Manage nationwide technical teams; conduct testing and quality assurance to ensure software products satisfy customer requirements.

Provide consulting services that integrate capacity and performance management studies into client-server environments.

84

Senior Systems Engineer, Halbern and Associates, Arlington, Virginia, 1991 - 1992

Managed performance component of requirements analysis of a major IRS systems project. Analyzed the functional requirements, defined the functional workloads, related workloads to Natural Work Units, defined data flows, described generic hardware configurations, and sized the hardware.

Directed installation of the MICS performance database product at a USAF Computer Services Center. Set up the MICS environment and defined MVS, VM, and Unisys database components. Developed the data conversion program to convert Unisys data to MICS and incorporated USAF's capacity planning requirements into the MICS database.

Technical Services Specialist, Aspen Software Corp., Bethesda, Maryland, 1990 - 1991

Directed the Technical Support Department of a software marketing and development company with computer simulation and direct mail application products.

Oversaw pre-sales / post-sales support, customer need and requirement identification and resolution, new product concept development, and product quality assurance.

Senior Consultant, AML Systems Inc., Fairfax, Virginia, 1978 - 1990

Managed technical and administrative activities of systems management projects with a customer base of commercial and government organizations in the United States, Great Britain, France, and Italy.

Implemented software to capture and report IBM's SMF / RMF data, Honeywell's SCF data, Unisys Log Accounting and SIP data, and DEC / VAX Accounting data.

Developed PC-based applications interfaced with CASE tools which used software engineering techniques to evaluate application performance.

Performance Analyst, Fidelity, Inc., Gaithersburg, Maryland, 1977 - 1978

Directed studies utilizing simulation and analytical techniques for solving management planning problems. Analyzed and developed discrete hardware / software performance parameters.

Systems Analyst, American Management Systems, Fairfax, Virginia, 1974 - 1977
Programmer, HALDEN Laboratories, Bethesda, Maryland, 1972 - 1974
Hardware Digital Communications Specialist, U.S. Army, Vietnam, 1968 - 1972
Programmer, HALDEN Laboratories, Bethesda, Maryland, 1968

EDUCATION

George Mason University, Fairfax, Virginia; three years Business Management
Computer Learning Center, Sterling, Virginia; one-year Computer Programming

MARY SCOTT WHITE
Social Security # XXX-XX-XXXX
753 East Avenue
Rochester, New York 14617
(716) XXX-XXXX

OBJECTIVE

Skilled educator with six years of teaching experience seeks a full-time teaching position for grades kindergarten through six. Expertise in delivering hands-on science programs that consistently motivate students.

EDUCATION

Hamilton College, Clinton, New York
  Bachelor of Arts in Elementary Education, 1995

ENDORSEMENTS / CERTIFICATIONS

New York State, Collegiate Professional Certificate, Elementary Grades NK-8

American Red Cross, CPR certified

WORK EXPERIENCE

Monroe County Public Schools, Owens Elementary School, Rochester, New York
  ELEMENTARY TEACHER, 1995 - present

Teach elementary school classes in all subject areas for second and third grades. Create customized lesson plans with hands-on activities that meet the needs of different styles of learning.

Improve group learning skills by initiating and implementing cooperative learning processes.

Institute effective classroom management by establishing behavioral rules, consequences, and rewards.

Identify reading levels utilizing Running Records to group and target reading requirements for all students.

Team teach and plan integrated units with teachers for second and third grades.

Coordinate biannual field trips with an interest in science.

Design unique and interactive bulletin boards to reinforce lessons and engage students.

Teach special education students within the classroom. Modify curriculum for learning disabled, Attention Deficit Disorder (ADD), and Attention Deficit Hyperactivity Disorder (ADHD) students.

Assist first- through third-grade students participating in the Homework Club.

Participate in organizing, managing, and judging the school science fair.

The Learning Tree, Rochester, New York
  TEACHER, Summers 1994, 1995

Lead teacher of elementary school students in after-school program.

Planned and directed an eight-week full-time summer camp program for elementary school students. Recruited speakers, developed activities, and organized field trips.

Monroe County Public Schools, Lilac Academy, Rochester, New York
  STUDENT TEACHER, Spring Semester 1995

Implemented lesson plans and worked directly with diverse size groups in grades one and six. Interacted with other faculty members and parents in a positive manner.

PRACTICUM, Spring 1994

Observed and interacted with second-grade students both individually and in a group setting, including students in special needs classes and Reading Recovery.

Monroe County Public Schools, Sundew Elementary School, East Rochester, New York
  PRACTICUM, Spring 1994

Observed and interacted with fourth-grade students including those with special needs.

ADDITIONAL SKILLS AND TRAINING

Monroe County Public Schools Training
  Junior Great Books Workshop, Spring 2000
  Emergent Literacy, Fall 1999
  Attention Deficit Disorder Seminar, Fall 1998
  Project Slow Learners Reading and Language Course, Spring 1997
  Macintosh Computer, Fall 1996

Computer Skills
  Proficient with IBM PC, Macintosh, Microsoft Word, PowerPoint.

HONORS AND MEMBERSHIPS

Dean's List, Hamilton College, 1993, 1994, 1995

Who's Who in American Colleges and Universities

Sigma Xi Honor Sorority, Hamilton College

Monroe County Educators Association (MCEA)

National Teachers Association (NTA)

MATTHEW CLANCY
97 Lucky Lane
Cambridge, Massachusetts 02138
Work (617) XXX-XXXX   Home (617) XXX-XXXX
E-mail: MClancy@bbg.net

QUALIFICATIONS SUMMARY

Technical professional with an expertise in Internet technologies. Experienced project manager with a proven record in designing, implementing, and maintaining diverse networks.

Quick learner, easily adapting to new systems and applications. Creative and energetic performer, willing to assume new assignments from conception to delivery. Excellent organizational and communication skills.

TECHNICAL SKILLS

Hardware: Cisco Routers, FORE Systems ATM, Juniper Networks, Copper Edge, Redback, DSL.

Software: Microsoft Office Suite, Corel Office Suite, Lotus Notes, dBase, BASIC, Windows 3.x, FolioVIEWS, LANAlyzer for Windows, MapInfo, Compass, Catalyst GIS, Catalyst Connect, DNS, BIND.

Operating Systems: Windows 95 / 98 / NT, Solaris 2.x, UNIX, VMS, Novell Netware, DOS.

Routing Protocols: IP, BGP 4, ISIS, OSPF, RIP.

EXPERIENCE

BBG Technologies, Boston, Massachusetts, 1996 - present
INTERNET NETWORK ENGINEER V, 1999 - present

Design, document, and oversee implementation of the BBG Global Management Network for North America, Europe, and Asia Pacific Regions. Establish detailed implementation plans and direct Operations to ensure execution of Management Network upgrades and redesigns.

Assign and control all IP networks for new hubs being built in North America. Provide operational support for router configuration generation, IP address assignments, and troubleshooting OSPF routing issues.

Team with Operations for integration support of legacy networks.

INTERNET BACKBONE ENGINEER IV, 1998 - 1999

Designed, configured, managed installation, and maintained all customer backbone hubs built for the East and West Coasts of North America. Implemented all new technology upgrades to existing hubs for the East and West Regions.

Supported the Customer Install Group; provided initial equipment for hub requirements and installation, tracked customer growth, and deployed resources to match future needs.

Managed daily activities for West Coast Region. Supervised a staff of four.

SYSTEMS ENGINEER, 1996 - 1998

Managed new and upgrade customer accounts from initial order through installation for router and CSU / DSU configuration and shipment, IP Network allocation, DNS Support, and domain registration / transition.

Extended feedback on Telco circuit installation, tested and accepted various Telco circuits, enabled IP routing, configured BGP routing, and supplied configuration information for customer Internet access.

Acted as a liaison with product development to test and evaluate new services.

Lockheed-Martin, Reston, Virginia, 1995 - 1996
SYSTEMS ENGINEER, 1995 - 1996

Provided a full range of engineering services including requirements analysis, test plan development, operations, and maintenance support for customers in the classified environment.

Administered diverse network systems, integrating varying operating platforms such as Novell Netware, Windows NT, UNIX, and DOS.

Celestial Inc., Boston, Massachusetts, 1992 - 1995
SENIOR TECHNICAL SUPPORT REPRESENTATIVE, 1992 - 1995

Extended technical support to clients on software and hardware issues.

Resolved in-house and client inquiries in person and via telephone concerning systems operation of DOS-based PCs, CD-ROM devices, Ccmail, Microsoft Word, Compass (demographic application), and Novell Netware 3.1x 250 node system. Diagnosed system hardware, software, and operator problems, recommending or performing minor remedial actions.

Performed daily Beta Tests of new software, debugging, and documentation.

Conducted classroom training for customers on Compass System.

XYZ Corporation, Stamford, Connecticut, 1990 - 1992
CUSTOMER/CONTRACT ADMINISTRATOR, 1990 - 1992

Furnished ADP integration services for state government negotiated contracts. Applied knowledge of contract administration; edited government proposals.

EDUCATION

Boston College, Chestnut Hill, Massachusetts
Master of Science Information Systems, 1995; Bachelor of Science in Business Administration, concentration Personnel Management and Computer Science, 1990

CERTIFICATIONS

Certified Netware Engineer
Certified Netware 3.1x and 4.1 Administrator

Handling Résumés Electronically

3

Self-Test Your Savvy in Delivering Your Résumé Electronically: Will Your Electronic Résumé Be Legible When It Arrives?

The following self-test is a tool to help you assess your readiness in preparing and sending electronic résumés. The objective is not to get the highest score possible, but to pinpoint areas that you can strengthen to help you prepare and mail an electronic résumé that a prospective employer will find easy to read.

1. Mailing a résumé electronically is the quickest way to send a résumé.   T/F __
2. Employers prefer to receive résumés via electronic mail.   T/F __
3. I can just send the résumé I've prepared in word processing as an attachment.   T/F __
4. It's best to send my résumé in MIME format so it will get there even quicker.   T/F __
5. Each line of text should have no more than 75 characters.   T/F __
6. I should use a fixed-width font.   T/F __
7. Cover letters are important but I should include one only if requested when transmitting an electronic résumé.   T/F __
8. Electronic résumés use left justification.   T/F __
9. I can just use my traditional résumé and send it through my electronic mail program.   T/F __

10. Each succeeding page of my electronic résumé does not
    need my name and page number.   T/F __

11. I shouldn't use bold and bullets when mailing electronically.   T/F __

12. It's best to balance my résumé with uppercase and normal
    capitalization.   T/F __

13. Electronic résumés read best with centered section headings.   T/F __

14. I can't use italics in my electronic résumé.   T/F __

15. My electronic résumé should be no more than one to
    two pages.   T/F __

16. Electronic mail programs are compatible.   T/F __

17. I should send my résumé as an attachment only when asked.   T/F __

18. Any organization that provides an electronic mail address
    would like you to transmit your résumé electronically.   T/F __

19. Each organization has its own guidelines for résumé
    delivery and I should follow each requirement carefully.   T/F __

Total: _____

Score 1 point for each "True" response and 0 for each "False" response, EXCEPT for questions 2, 3, 4, 9, 13, 15, 16, 18. *For these questions only,* **subtract** 1 point for each "True" response. Record your total. A score below +9 indicates that you would benefit from practicing the electronic résumé-writing techniques discussed in this chapter. (*Note:* It is possible to have a negative score.)

Electronic Résumé Fundamentals

Organizations lose productivity when positions remain vacant. Technology has now provided employers and recruiters new tools to expedite the recruitment and hiring process, enabling quicker access and evaluation of job applicants and their qualifications.

Some organizations are utilizing electronic mail as a delivery option for résumés. Many recruiters prefer to receive résumés electronically because it moves applicants quickly through the hiring process; they either scan the document visually or send it on for computer scanning, electronically forwarding to hiring managers those résumés that meet job requirements.

Other organizations request job seekers visit their Web site and complete applications online. Applicants are directed to complete a number of fields and insert a plain text résumé.

Plain text or ASCII is the text of choice for résumés transmitted electronically or via the Internet. ASCII bridges the gap between the multitude of word-processing and electronic mail programs because it is universally recognized by personal computers, Macintosh computers, UNIX workstations, and mainframe terminals.

But not all organizations are either set up or want to receive their résumés or applications in electronic format, so you must identify and comply with organizational requirements before you apply.

When to Send an Electronic Résumé

You'll prepare and send a résumé in plain text or ASCII when:

1. A hiring manager or recruiter requests one.
2. A newspaper employment listing states you should forward your résumé and provides an electronic mail (e-mail) address.
3. An organization requests on its Web site that you use its e-mail address to deliver your résumé.
4. An organization provides an online form on its Web site to quickly forward your résumé and cover letter in ASCII text.

in Electronic Résumés

Electronic résumés start out as either traditional or scannable résumés, so you'll use the appropriate content from your traditional or scannable résumé.

in Electronic Résumés

1. Don't use an electronic mail address from work; use a personal electronic mail address.
2. Avoid unprofessional-sounding screen names. Remember, when employers open their electronic mail, they see a listing with the subject and sender. It is more appropriate to send a message from Sambates@abc.com rather than Poodlelover@abc.com.

Tip: Choose black text only. Color text will take longer to transmit and may be unreadable.

in Electronic Résumés

- STEP 1: Evaluate the job you are seeking and locate the job requirements.
- STEP 2: Determine if you have an existing résumé on file that meets the criteria.
- STEP 3: If your résumé meets the criteria, follow the directions under "Formatting Electronic Résumés."
- STEP 4: If your résumé does not demonstrate that you meet the job requirements, save it as a new document and work through each section, detailing skills, experience, education, training, and credentials that match job specifications.

Tips on Writing Electronic Résumés

1. Prepare your résumé in your word-processing program and use the spelling checker.
2. Proof the electronic mail address, subject, and your electronic résumé carefully before sending. It is easy to hit the wrong keys when using electronic mail so carefully check for errors before transmitting.

Tip: Avoid transmitting your résumé in MIME (Multipurpose Internet Mail Extensions). Its purpose is transmission of nontext files, so résumés sent this way usually arrive illegible.

Special Situations

   ~ *The application requirements in the newspaper employment listing request that you e-mail a résumé in MS (Microsoft) Word format.* You must adhere to application requirements, so format your résumé using Microsoft Word and mail it electronically as an attachment. In all other instances, follow the directions detailed in "Producing Electronic Résumés."

   ~ *The résumé that arrived looks different from the résumé that was sent.* Format your résumé and send a copy to yourself or to a trusted friend or colleague. Correct any problems before transmitting it to an employer.

Formatting Electronic Résumés

How you format your résumé prior to transmittal determines how it will look when received. Follow the instructions carefully to ensure legibility.

* Use left justification for all text.
* Remove all special effects such as ruling lines, bullets, bold, italics, and underline.

- Use uppercase to emphasize section headings, job titles, organization names, colleges/universities, and degrees. (These are just examples; choose uppercase only for the items you want to highlight.)
- Balance spacing and uppercase to complement appearance and legibility. Space text carefully for clarity.
- Set your right hand margin to 6 or 6.5 inches to ensure no more than 75 characters per line. This should eliminate the problem of premature line wraps.
- Convert all text to ASCII.
- Save the entire document as a text file.

Producing Electronic Résumés

When you are ready to mail your résumé electronically, follow these steps:

- STEP 1: Copy your résumé using the pull-down edit menu.
- STEP 2: Open your electronic mail program.
- STEP 3: Select "compose a message."
- STEP 4: Fill in the address section with the e-mail address of your recipient.
- STEP 5: Use the subject area to state what you are sending, for example: "Résumé for Billing Supervisor" or "IT Manager Résumé."
- STEP 6: Paste your résumé into the body of the e-mail message.
- STEP 7: Review the message to ensure adequate spacing, no premature line breaks, and ease in readability.
- STEP 8: Send your message.

Tip: Send a copy of your electronic résumé to yourself, print it out, and evaluate its visual appearance.

Sample Electronic Résumé

The following is a sample electronic résumé.

SALLIE MAE LEE
715 West Hawthorne Avenue
Winston-Salem, North Carolina 27100
Work (919) XXX-XXXX
Home (919) XXX-XXXX

QUALIFICATIONS SUMMARY

Dedicated and results-oriented professional with progressive administrative experience. Excellent communication, organization, and interpersonal skills. Computer savvy with an expertise in word processing, spreadsheet, scheduling, presentation, mail, and Internet applications.

SKILLS

Proficient in Windows 98, Microsoft Word, Excel, Access, and PowerPoint.

EXPERIENCE

Southern Applications, Inc., Winston-Salem, North Carolina
EXECUTIVE ASSISTANT, 1996 - present

Assist executive of a software manufacturer with annual sales of $40 million. Prioritize and assign tasks to sales staff; monitor progress and status of departmental projects.

Schedule and arrange travel, meetings, and training. Collaborate with senior-level sales managers to plan and conduct trade shows, exhibits, and customer conferences.

Act as liaison with corporate partners and product resellers to distribute pricing updates. Resolve customer inquiries for product information, purchasing, and pricing.

Point of contact with building management, MIS, accounts payable, and office equipment contractors to facilitate smooth office operations.

Track and reconcile revenue to ensure accurate commission statements.

The Mason Group, Atlanta, Georgia
ADMINISTRATIVE ASSISTANT, OFFICE MANAGER, 1994 - 1996

Managed administrative operations of a small public relations firm and supervised one staff member.

Assisted partners and associates with client projects by conducting research using diverse resources.

Produced monthly invoices and prepared reports detailing client billings and expenditures.

Created and maintained an extensive library of public relations resources.

Managed a LAN and expanded program applications.

City of Charleston, Charleston, South Carolina
OFFICE AUTOMATION ASSISTANT, 1993 - 1994
PROCUREMENT CLERK, CLERK-TYPIST,
Summers and School Breaks, 1990 - 1993

Provided assistance to the Director of Electronic Commerce. Prepared briefing materials for meetings and presentations given to senior-level government officials including the City Manager and the Controller.

Recognized with On-the-Spot Award, letter of appreciation from City Manager John T. Public, and the Controller's Performance Review Excellence Award.

EDUCATION

B.A. in Sociology, 1993
Charleston Southern University, Charleston, South Carolina

PART TWO

Covering All Bases—
Cover Letters

Writing Effective Cover Letters

4

Self-Test Your Savvy in Writing Job Search Letters: How Good Are You at Communicating on Paper?

The following self-test is a tool to help you assess your readiness in writing letters. The objective is not to get the highest score possible, but to pinpoint areas that you can strengthen to help you write and produce letters that will effectively market and position you for the jobs you pursue.

1. I must direct my letters to specific individuals.   T/F __
2. If I can't locate the name of an individual, I can use the old standby "To Whom it May Concern."   T/F __
3. When using a letter with my résumé, I should include specific information about my qualifications and experience that targets my credentials for the job I am seeking.   T/F __
4. Employers will evaluate my written communication skills based on my correspondence.   T/F __
5. Letters should be one to two pages long.   T/F __
6. I should avoid beginning too many sentences with the pronoun "I."   T/F __
7. Great letters won't get me a job but they'll get me an interview.   T/F __
8. Most hiring managers don't even read letters but go right to the résumé.   T/F __

9. It doesn't matter if the fonts of a letter and résumé match,
   but it's nice if they do.   T/F __

10. I should buy extra paper when printing my résumés so all
    of my job search letters will be on the same paper.   T/F __

11. Written communication skills are highly prized, so a
    well-written letter will capture attention.   T/F __

12. If I put a great deal of effort into crafting my job search
    letters, I can continue to customize and modify them
    throughout my job search.   T/F __

13. Handwritten correspondence is fine for some types of
    job search correspondence.   T/F __

14. "Please call me at your earliest convenience" is a
    strong close.   T/F __

15. A comma is the appropriate punctuation to use after
    the salutation.   T/F __

16. Only the first word is capitalized in the complimentary close. T/F __

17. If I choose a font for my letter that looks like handwriting,
    it will appear more personal and be well received by the
    recipient.   T/F __

18. Letters should be double-spaced.   T/F __

19. Recipients will be more likely to open an envelope with
    a name and address that is either handwritten or typewritten. T/F __

20. I will get a better response if I customize my letters
    rather than do a mass mailing.   T/F __

21. I'll need a cover sheet for my cover letter when
    transmitting via facsimile.   T/F __

22. It's okay to fax all types of job search correspondence.   T/F __

23. Some types of job search correspondence can be
    transmitted via electronic mail.   T/F __

24. If an organization does not send me an offer letter,
    it is in my best interest to send one.   T/F __

25. I should send thank-you letters for every job interview.   T/F __

26. Many job seekers overlook the importance of
    correspondence in their job search.   T/F __

27. Wise job seekers customize letters for almost every job inquiry. T/F __

28. I will leave a good impression if I write a letter that expresses appreciation when I decide to decline an offer. T/F __

29. I should use follow-up letters to pursue interesting opportunities, but I must be creative in my approach so I don't become a pest. T/F __

30. Thank-you letters are appropriate for anyone who has helped me during my job search. T/F __

31. Offer letters confirm the position, start date, salary, salary range, and benefits. T/F __

32. It is essential that all correspondence be error-free. T/F __

33. If I make a mistake, it is okay to use correction fluid. T/F __

34. Electronic correspondence has the same formality as written correspondence. T/F __

35. The tone of all my job search correspondence should be positive and upbeat. T/F __

Total: _____

Score 1 point for each "True" response and 0 for each "False" response, EXCEPT for questions 2, 5, 8, 14, 15, 17, 18, 21, 22, 33, 34. *For these questions only*, **subtract** 1 point for each "True" response. Record your total. A score below +22 indicates that you would benefit from practicing the letter-writing techniques discussed in this chapter. (*Note:* It is possible to have a negative score.)

Why Use Letters in the Job Search?

Job search letters are business letters directed at prospective employers and your network that indicate your interest in employment, appreciation for interviews and support, confirmation or refusal of job offers, and termination of current positions.

Job search letters tell a prospective employer a lot about you, both by what you choose to include and exclude and whether you pay attention to detail. It shows how professional you are and how well you communicate.

Hiring managers use job search letters to screen likely candidates from the unlikely. They always accompany your résumé, serving to introduce it. Résumés that arrive without a letter are rarely read, so think of your letter and résumé as a team.

An enticing letter encourages the employer to review your credentials and read your résumé. If your letter doesn't tempt the reader, your qualifications may not get a second glance.

You can often use the same résumé for several jobs, but your letters must be tailored and directed for each specific job search situation and position so the reader thinks it was written solely for him or her. Optimally, each letter should reflect how your qualifications fit and mesh with the requirements for each job you seek.

Letter Parts

Your letters must follow accepted business letter principles and formats. Your letter set-up—space between elements, paragraph indents, placement of addresses, salutations, and closes—must be consistent and clear because you don't want to give an employer any reason to discard your letter and your résumé. Figure 4–1 shows all the basic elements.

I. WRITER'S ADDRESS

The sender's name, street address, city, state, ZIP Code, and phone number, typed with single spacing.

2. DATE

The month, day, and year the letter is typed.

3. INSIDE ADDRESS

The name of the person to whom you are writing, company, his or her job title, street address, city, state, and ZIP Code, typed with single spacing.

4. SALUTATION

The opening greeting, such as "Dear Ms. Miller," followed with a colon.

5. BODY OF LETTER

The text or message of the letter, usually five to six paragraphs, typed with single spacing using a double space between paragraphs.

6. COMPLIMENTARY CLOSE

A closing phrase such as "Very truly yours" or "Sincerely yours."

7. WRITER'S IDENTIFICATION

The sender's (and signer's) full name.

8. ENCLOSURE

A reminder that an enclosure is included.

1. Writer's address		28 Liberty Street
		Pontiac, MI 48341
		(313) XXX-XXXX

(Spacing varies, usually 2–4 spaces)

2. Date	November 14, 20XX

(4 spaces)

Mr. John Jones
Personnel Director   **3. Inside address**
ABC Company
85 Main Street
Pontiac, MI 48341

(2 spaces)

Dear Mr. Jones: **4. Salutation**

(2 spaces)

5. Body of letter

Peter Smith suggested I contact you concerning your search for a Director of Public Relations. My six years of progressive public relations experience qualifies me for this position.

(2 spaces)

I have worked with both nonprofit and corporate organizations, developing an expertise in cultivating local and national media contacts.

(2 spaces)

New projects and ideas are particularly exciting to me and I enjoy transforming concepts into reality. Additionally, I have excellent interpersonal and management skills, interfacing effectively at all organizational levels.

(2 spaces)

I am interested in the challenge your position presents and would like to meet with you to discuss my credentials and your requirements. I look forward to speaking with you.

(2 spaces)

6. Complimentary close	Sincerely yours,

(4 spaces)

7. Writer's identification	Dillon Thompson

(2 spaces)

Encl.   **8. Enclosure notation**

Figure 4–1. Basic business letter set-up.

Letter Format

The most appropriate business letter formats are the block, semiblock, and semiblock indented. All three are acceptable, and the choice is yours. Examples of these are shown in Figure 4–2.

Full Block

All text is set flush against the left-hand margin.

_____

_____

_____

_____

_____

_____

_____

_____:

_____

_____

_____

_____

_____,

_____

Figure 4–2. The three business letter formats.

Figure 4–2 *(continued)*

Semiblock

The date and writer's address usually align at the center of the page. The complimentary close and the writer's name align under the address.

_____
_____
_____

_____

_____
_____
_____

_____:

_____
_____

_____
_____

_____,

_____

Figure 4–2 *(continued)*

Semiblock Indented

The date, writer's address, complimentary close, and the writer's name are set on a tab and align with each other. The first line of each paragraph is also indented.

_____

_____

_____

_____

_____

_____

_____

_____:

_____

_____

_____

_____

_____,

_____

General Guidelines

1. Type all letters; handwritten letters are unacceptable. A personnel specialist once showed me a letter and résumé she had received— written in calligraphy. Commenting on the letter's beauty, she said she wished she had a need for a calligrapher. However, neither of us bothered to review the text to see what kind of job the applicant was seeking.

2. Use single spacing for the text and double spacing between paragraphs.

3. To achieve a professional and neat appearance, use full justification; this produces even margins by aligning the text at the right as well as the left. Many word-processing programs let you hyphenate words that don't fit. Hyphenation can be turned on or off. Consult your reference manual and choose your preference.

4. Allow one-inch margins at top, bottom, and sides of the letter. For a balanced, sleek look, use your software's "center page" feature to center the text vertically between the top and bottom margins.

5. Address each letter to a specific individual, and include his or her name and job title in the inside address. If you are sending an unsolicited letter, research at the library, call the company, or check out its Web site to find out to whom to send it. If you are responding to a classified advertisement that does not include the name of the person to send it to, call the organization and identify the recipient. Above all else, make sure to spell the person's name correctly and use his or her correct title.

6. If you don't know what courtesy title a woman prefers, use Ms. If you are unable to determine the individual's gender, omit the courtesy title and begin the letter like this:

   Lee Smith:

     or

   Dear Lee Smith:

7. Date and sign the letter.

Tip: Always write the month in full, never abbreviating or using figures.

8. Include your telephone number (don't forget the area code), either in the return address or in your closing paragraph, or both.
9. Abbreviate the state name on both the inside and outside address, using acceptable post office abbreviations. But it is permissible either to spell out or to abbreviate the state name on your letterhead. Remember, state names are always spelled out in the text of your letter. Consult the following list for the abbreviations recommended by the U.S. Postal Service.

Tip: The U.S. Postal Service state abbreviations must be used with ZIP Codes.

U.S. POSTAL SERVICE ABBREVIATIONS

AL	Alabama	MT	Montana
AK	Alaska	NE	Nebraska
AR	Arkansas	NH	New Hampshire
AZ	Arizona	NV	Nevada
CA	California	NJ	New Jersey
CZ	Canal Zone	NM	New Mexico
CO	Colorado	NY	New York
CT	Connecticut	NC	North Carolina
DE	Delaware	ND	North Dakota
DC	District of Columbia	OH	Ohio
FL	Florida	OK	Oklahoma
GA	Georgia	OR	Oregon
GU	Guam	PA	Pennsylvania
HI	Hawaii	PR	Puerto Rico
ID	Idaho	RI	Rhode Island
IL	Illinois	SC	South Carolina
IN	Indiana	SD	South Dakota
IA	Iowa	TN	Tennessee
KS	Kansas	TX	Texas
KY	Kentucky	UT	Utah

LA	Louisiana	VT	Vermont
ME	Maine	VA	Virginia
MD	Maryland	VI	Virgin Islands
MA	Massachusetts	WA	Washington
MI	Michigan	WV	West Virginia
MN	Minnesota	WI	Wisconsin
MS	Mississippi	WY	Wyoming
MO	Missouri		

10. Include the following notation when enclosing items:

> Enclosure
> Encl.
> or
> Enc.

If more than one enclosure is included, specify the number:

> Enclosures (2)

11. Follow basic rules for numbers. It is usual to spell out numbers from 1 through 10, using numerals for 11 and over. Always spell out a number that begins a sentence. Be consistent and follow the same style—for related numbers—in a paragraph. Check for special rules in a business-writing reference book.

12. Consult reference books, dictionaries, and thesauruses for rules on grammar, usage, business-writing principles, word choice, and spelling.

Production Tips

Presentation is as important as content. Let's consider a number of factors.

1. Your letter must be produced on a computer with word-processing software. You can make changes easily, make the letter graphically interesting, and store the information for further use.

2. Select a print style (font) that is easy to read and professional in appearance. Avoid script, italics, Old English, calligraphy, or any print type that is unprofessional or detracts from your content. Make sure the type size is readable. While it is common to use 10- and 12-point type for a résumé, a cover letter is a business letter, so use the standard 12-point type.

Tip: While résumé and letter fonts are not required to match, they look professional if they do.

---

3. You'll achieve a very professional appearance by producing your cover letters and résumés on the same paper. Choose $8^1/_2 \times 11$-inch 24-pound paper, 100 percent rag (best quality) or 25 percent rag (good quality). Stationery supply stores and copy/print shops carry a wide range of paper and envelopes. I tend to be conservative when it comes to color and recommend white, off-white, buff, cream, ivory, or beige. Avoid marbled, mottled paper, regardless of color; it's hard to read and photocopies poorly (employers often make photocopies of cover letters to distribute to other hiring managers).

4. Personalized stationery gives your cover letters a very polished, professional look. You can create your own business letterhead for your letters if you have access to desktop publishing or word-processing software with desktop-publishing capabilities. Another option is to center your address and phone number at the top of the page.

5. Purchase envelopes that match your paper, but use them only for sending your follow-up letters, thank-you notes, resignation, and offer/decline letters. To ensure that your résumé and cover letter arrive unfolded and unwrinkled, send them in a 9×12-inch envelope.

The Content

Here is a standard letter format that you can adjust for each job search purpose by modifying the format, organization, and special effects.

- *1st paragraph:* The introductory or opening paragraph states the purpose of your letter. Are you responding to an employment advertisement? Are you thanking the employer for a job interview? Did someone refer you to the organization? Are you intrigued by its products or services? Arouse the reader's interest now, and he or she will want to read further.

- *2nd paragraph:* This transitional paragraph expands on your opening by including or reinforcing your experience, education/training, and other credentials that meet job requirements or support employment with this organization.

- *3rd paragraph:* Here you can familiarize the reader with your accomplishments, such as increased membership or decreased expenditures. Use a sentence or two to explain how you fit the position and what you'll bring to it, for example, enthusiasm, dedication, or commitment.

- *4th paragraph:* This paragraph ties into the first by restating your interest in the organization and/or position, stating your availability, making a request to meet or speak about the job or opportunities, or confirming your interest in the position and organization.

Once your letter is roughed out, edit, rewrite, and reorganize your sentences until you're satisfied with their clarity and construction. Check for grammatical errors, redundancies, misspelled words, and overall accuracy.

Punctuation

Proper punctuation separates your words into sentences, phrases, and clauses, making your letters easier to read and understand.

- Use a **colon** (:) after a word that introduces a quotation or a list of items, and the salutation in a letter.

- Use a **comma** (,) when a natural pause indicates a slight separation of ideas.

- Use a **semicolon** (;) to separate independent clauses when a coordinating conjunction (and, but, or, nor) is absent.

- Use a **period** (.) to end a complete declarative sentence.
- Use a **question mark** (?) to end a direct question.
- Use a **hyphen** (-) to connect the elements of certain compound words.
- Use **quotation marks** (" ") to emphasize special words or phrases, such as names of awards; denote someone's exact words; indicate the titles of chapters and sections in published works; and highlight the titles of unpublished manuscripts, dissertations, and reports.

Tip: If you are having difficulty using proper grammar, get some help by brushing up with either a book, course or workshop, or online tutorial program.

Frequently Misspelled Words

Any mistake, whether it concerns spelling, grammar, punctuation, or poor word choice, can knock you out of the running. You've spent too much time and effort writing your letter to lose out because of errors. If your computer software has a spelling checker, use it. But don't rely on it; it will bypass words that are spelled correctly but are not the correct word. For example, if you mistakenly type in *manger* instead of *manager*, the spelling checker will accept *manger*. Watch out for the following words frequently misspelled in cover letters:

achieve	experience	pursue
advertisement	immediately	schedule
benefit	judgment	sincerely
business	knowledge	succeed
challenge (challenging)	opportunity	success
develop	parallel	successfully
excellent	performance	truly

Tip: Proofread, proofread, proofread! I cannot stress enough the importance of preparing and sending error-free letters.

Putting Your Job Search Letters to Work

5

With your job search letters in hand, ensure the best results by developing a strategy for using them. Decide how much, or what percentage, of your time you'll direct to finding job opportunities. For example: 40 percent for networking, 25 percent for referrals, 10 percent for advertisements, and 25 percent for direct applications.

You'll get the best results if you set goals for your search and devise a way to organize yourself, designing a strategy that suits your needs and job search goals. The following steps will help you organize your job search:

- STEP 1: Keep a record of every letter you mail, including such information as date mailed, company or box number, contact name, phone number, follow-up dates (several columns), and results. Log in every letter sent, whether it's a response to an advertisement, referral, or unsolicited letter.

- STEP 2: Print extra copies or make photocopies of every letter you send and store them in file folders (labeled for each type of letter) or a three-ring binder. When you respond to an advertisement from the Internet, newspaper, or professional journal, attach the announcement to your photocopy.

- STEP 3: Schedule mailings to fit your daily routine. Try mailing responses to the advertisements on one particular day, and unsolicited and referral letters on another.

- STEP 4: If you're doing a bulk mailing and you think it will take you two weeks to complete it, date all the letters with the future completion date. Mail all letters together when completed.

Tip: If you mail a letter to yourself, you'll have an idea of when your letters reached their destination.

- STEP 5: Always follow up a letter with a phone call after you allow the letter a day or two to travel through the office mail system.

The Post-Letter Follow-Up Call

I have seen so many people exert great effort seeking out job leads, researching potential employers, writing and mailing dozens of letters only to stagnate in the job search because they failed to follow up their letters with a phone call. Don't make the same mistake.

The success of your job search is directly correlated to how well you follow up your letters. Employers do not have the time or the interest to follow up every letter they receive. So it is in your best interest to follow up every letter you send with a phone call requesting a personal meeting or interview.

Consider preparing a script because these phone calls aren't easy to make. You will be more relaxed if you know in advance what you want to say. Here's an example you can modify to meet your needs:

> "Hello, Mr. Smith. This is Robbie Kaplan. I'm following up on a letter I sent you last week concerning job opportunities within your organization."
>
> *(Pause . . . give him a chance to respond.)*
>
> "I'd like to set up an appointment with you to discuss my qualifications and your needs."
>
> *(Pause.)*

If Mr. Smith says "no thanks," try to get something positive out of the exchange. For instance, you could ask him if he knows of any job opportunities inside or outside his organization or if he could recommend someone with knowledge about job openings. Remember, nothing ventured, nothing gained. Follow-up phone calls are a great way to get referrals, and it's a lot easier to contact someone when you can say, "Mr. Smith suggested I give you a call concerning accounting opportunities."

Apply these steps for follow-up success:

- STEP 1: It's most effective to make at least ten calls at a time.

- STEP 2: Develop a rhythm when making a number of calls and you'll become more confident and at ease the more calls you make.

- STEP 3: Begin with the least risky/least wanted jobs and employers and save jobs or contacts of greatest interest for last.

- STEP 4: Each individual you reach and each successful encounter will buoy your spirits.

- STEP 5: If you make your calls either between 8:00 and 8:30 in the morning or between 5:00 and 6:00 in the evening, you'll catch more people at their desks.

- STEP 6: If you reach a secretary and find the contact is not available, advise him or her that you'll call back. Or, leave your name and number and say explicitly that you're following up on correspondence with Mr. Smith.

- STEP 7: If you reach some type of voice mail or answering machine, leave a message detailing your name, that you're following up on correspondence, that you'd like a return call, and where you can be reached.

Tip: If you don't receive a return call within one week, place another phone call. People are busy and don't always give these types of calls priority.

Turning Possibilities into Opportunities

The most successful job searches are directed with positive thinking. You can turn negatives into positives by being as proactive and persistent as possible. For example, if a department or division turns you down and you're still interested, locate a hiring manager or individual in another division.

If you've heard of an appealing job or seen one advertised, and, for whatever reason, the fit is not quite right, you can contact the organization anyway and offer your services in another capacity as in the example shown on page 120.

Joanna Joseph
_____

54 West 73rd Street
New York, New York 10003
(212) XXX-XXXX

February 10, 20XX

College Books, Inc.
10 Broadway
12th Floor
New York, NY 10038

Dear Ms. Williams:

Although I do not have experience for the Managing Editor position you advertised in *The New York Times*, I am interested in becoming a freelance writer for your company.

As an educator and writer, I developed a wide variety of training programs and workshops for diverse audiences. I also wrote successful grant proposals, researched and created innovative curriculum projects, and generated and gathered pertinent information for annual program evaluation reports.

Most recently, I wrote a health textbook for second-grade students. The enclosed résumé highlights my accomplishments.

I would like the opportunity to meet with you to discuss my credentials and your requirements.

Sincerely,

Joanna Joseph

Encl.

ABC Company
67th Highway
Fort Lauderdale, FL 33395

January 2, 20XX

Ms. Rosalind Thompson
Health Care USA
7880 Sunny Boulevard
Fort Lauderdale, FL 33394

Dear Ms. Thompson:

I want to give you my recommendation for Larry Long, who is an employee with ABC Company. Mr. Long is a purchasing agent at Headquarters in Fort Lauderdale, Florida.

Mr. Long has been a member of ABC's purchasing staff since January XXXX. I have found him to be an extremely competent and conscientious employee and feel he would be an asset to any organization.

The purchasing program entails working with several hospitals to establish common purchasing programs in medical supplies through national contracts and dealing with miscellaneous bulk purchases outside of the medical supplies area. Mr. Long's interpersonal skills and knowledge of purchasing and negotiation have been valuable in performing these tasks.

I regret that due to ABC Company's effort to reduce a large budget deficit, I have been forced to terminate Mr. Long's employment as part of an overall staff cutback.

If you have any questions about Mr. Long's abilities to assist your organization, please contact me at (407) XXX-XXXX.

Sincerely,

Marsha Mitt
General Manager

MM/jk

Being proactive is a good way of dealing with a pending layoff. If your organization is downsizing and you're facing a layoff, ask your immediate supervisor to write you a letter of introduction. Many organizations, faced with terminating qualified individuals, are willing not only to write letters but direct and address them to appropriate organizations.

These letters (see the example on page 121) are written on your employer's stationery, and either you or your employer supplies the organizations and contact names. If your employer plans to address them "To Whom It May Concern," ask if they can be personalized if you supply names and addresses.

Using Electronic Letters

6

Electronic mail is easy, direct, and fast, and it's revolutionizing the way professionals communicate. It's less formal and cheaper than a letter, easier than sending a fax, but more formal and less intrusive than a conversation. Yet it appears almost conversational because the recipient can respond or ask questions immediately. Because electronic mail can be transmitted 24 hours a day, 7 days a week, it transcends time zones, opening unlimited communication.

Professionals like using electronic mail (e-mail) and it has become a standard form of business communication, often preferred over voice mail. Many individuals find they are more effective when communicating in writing, and electronic mail allows them time to mull over a message and respond with more substance than a telephone conversation.

Not surprising, recruiters for technology-driven organizations were the first to use electronic mail in the recruitment process, primarily for résumé delivery. It proved to be a quick way to scan potential applicants, respond immediately to job seekers on the status of their candidacy, and forward résumés to hiring managers. Now that electronic mail is a common communication vehicle for both private and public sectors and used across industries, it has become an effective employment tool for both recruiters and job seekers.

According to job seekers and recruiters, electronic mail allows direct submission to a greater number of recipients. Messages are quickly delivered to recipients, often within minutes of their transmission, making it the quickest and also the least expensive communication vehicle. Job seekers can communicate specifics about their experience, thank the individuals with whom they interviewed, and officially accept employment. But, electronic mail is just one of several communication options and people should carefully weigh when it is most appropriate to use it, mail or fax a letter or résumé, or communicate verbally.

Some fast-growing companies, often in the technology industry, are implementing organization-wide electronic recruiting programs that rely solely on the Internet and electronic mail to recruit applicants. They're establishing recruitment Web sites with recruiting pages that educate people with detailed job descriptions, application procedures, and organization information. They even post recruitment ads on selected and targeted Web sites to attract applicants who not only have the skills, experience, and training backgrounds they seek, but meet hobby and interest profiles of current employees.

Electronic Letter Parts

1. TO

The "To" section is the screen name, user name, or e-mail address of the intended recipient. Check your recipient's electronic mail address carefully to ensure accuracy. Verify message delivery by checking your electronic mail regularly and scan for nondeliverable or returned mail error messages.

2. CC

The "CC" section allows you to forward a copy of your message to another individual. Just include the screen name, user name, or e-mail address of the intended recipient and he or she will receive a copy of your message.

3. SUBJECT

The "Subject Box" is the primary indicator your recipient receives that gives a clue to your message. It's important to make your subject direct and of interest as individuals screen their messages and may delete any they conclude has no relevance. Make sure not to leave the subject box empty because your recipient may assume your message is junk mail if there is no subject.

Tip: Don't just put anything in the subject box; rather, use it to clarify what the message is about, making it stand out without being cute or a ruse. If you are responding to a job advertisement or announcement, use a major skill as an eye-catcher, such as "COBOL Programmer," "UNIX, NT Technical Analyst," or "Employee Communication Manager." Other choices would be "Credit Manager Position," "Résumé for Facilities Manager" or "Résumé of Mary Sharp."

---

4. BODY OF MESSAGE

This is where the text of your message appears. Recruiters and hiring managers use your message to evaluate your ability to communicate, so it is crucial that your electronic message presents you professionally, both grammatically and visually.

When to Send an Electronic Letter

If you're like most people who are tired of leaving phone messages that seldom get answered, electronic mail offers an alternative to one of the biggest barriers of the job search. While many professionals have others screen their mail and phone calls, executives and human resource professionals actually read their electronic mail. You'll be surprised at how many contacts you can reach, and their responses should expedite your job search.

Use e-mail to:

1. Prospect in your network for opportunities, potential organizations, or contacts.
2. Make initial contact with hiring managers or employees in organizations of interest.
3. Respond to positions of interest that request an electronic mail response.
4. Thank individuals after an interview or for job-search assistance.

5. Follow up on positions of interest.
6. Initiate contact with referrals.
7. Accept or decline offers that have been extended through electronic mail.

General Guidelines

1. While electronic mail is less formal than written correspondence, it is just as permanent as a written document. The recipient will know you only by what you say and how well you say it. Make a strong first impression with a clear, concise, easy-to-read, and properly formatted message using correct spelling, grammar, and punctuation.
2. Don't think that because electronic mail is more immediate and personable that it should be personal. Business communications are business messages and they require a certain degree of formality.
3. If you are currently employed, you probably have electronic mail through your employer and are comfortable using it. It is absolutely essential that you have your own Internet connection and corresponding electronic mail program and address while searching for a job as it is inappropriate to use your current employer's.
4. The most important point to get across in your message is how your qualifications match the position you seek and how well you understand the actual qualifications for that specific job, such as travel, education, experience, salary requirements, or eligibility to work in the United States.
5. All electronic mail programs require a user or screen name; some programs allow you to choose several. Make sure you select a professional user name for the job search, preferably your name. The hiring manager's or recruiter's "in box" shows a listing of messages with only the sender's user name and subject. While you may be a fanatic gardener, a recruiter is likely to pass over a message from Iluvgardening@abc.com or other unprofessional names when it arrives in the "in box."
6. Electronic messages should contain all of the information your recipient needs, keeping the message both short and direct.

Tip: Avoid flowery statements while highlighting your qualifications or interests; the hiring manager will judge that later.

7. Explain yourself right away, telling the employer what he or she needs to know, writing a succinct message that uses the fewest words. While watching your word count, beware of being too brief and not communicating both your qualifications and interests.
8. Because electronic mail is a less formal means of communication, there are no firm rules on how to either open or close your messages. Avoid using a salutation or a closing that is too casual for business correspondence.
9. Recipients are comfortable with messages that either use just their courtesy title and last name, for example, "Ms. Smith" or "Mr. Williams," or begin with "Dear Ms. James."

Tip: If you know the name but the gender is in doubt or you don't know someone's preference, use "Dear Kelly Thomson."

10. You can take your cue from a correspondent when replying to a message. If the person uses both first and last names, it is appropriate to address that person formally. If the person has signed the message with only the first name, you can address the person accordingly.
11. Electronic mail is a form of business communication and requires the same proper use of language as written letters. If in doubt, refer to a grammar or style guide.
12. It's important to close your electronic letters with your real name, not your screen name. You can just write in your first and last names or, depending on your electronic mail program capabilities, you can develop separate signatures that provide alternative ways to reach you, such as:

Betty Thomas
(212) XXX-XXXX voice
Bettythomas@abc.com

in Electronic Letters

- It's not professional or confidential to use your company electronic mail address during your job search.
- Craft your message carefully for the possibility of multiple recipients. Your recipient may forward it to other individuals, both inside and outside the organization.
- Don't believe that your messages will remain private. Every organization or the system's administrator can access any electronic message you've sent or deleted.
- No one likes unsolicited junk mail so don't do a mass mailing of a bland networking, application, or résumé correspondence that isn't targeted to demonstrate how you meet specific job qualifications.

Tips on Writing Electronic Letters

1. Assume that your worst enemy or any major newspaper has access to your electronic mail and be wary of what you include.
2. Confirm that your recipients use their electronic mail before sending them messages. Many professionals have electronic mail addresses and use them on their business cards and letterhead. An electronic mail address alone doesn't mean professionals regularly read or use electronic mail.
3. Make an excellent first impression because—unlike the telephone—electronic mail leaves a written record.
4. Plan what you want to say and how you'll say it. Take the time to think about your messages and responses and avoid replying too quickly.
5. Be extra careful in typing your message as it is easy to make a mistake. If your electronic mail program has a spelling checker, turn it on and use it. If you do not have a spelling checker, you may want to type important messages in a word-processing program and, after

carefully checking for spelling and grammatical errors, copy and paste in your electronic mail program.

6. Save a written copy of your electronic mail correspondence just in case your electronic file disappears.

7. Ensure that all correspondence is virus-free.

8. Send yourself the message prior to sending it to your intended recipients. This way you will be able to see how your message reads and is formatted.

9. Use caution in sending unsolicited attachments with your electronic mail message. Get prior approval from your recipients to ensure that they will accept them.

10. Don't assume that the message you prepare and send will look identical when it is received. Your software and hardware may be different from what your recipients use and your visual message may look quite different when it is received.

Special Situations

~ *You don't yet have an Internet account and e-mail address but still want to communicate electronically.* There are free e-mail programs, but you don't get something for nothing; these free e-mail programs all include advertising with every outgoing message. You will have to decide if a job search message that includes banners of advertising is the image you want to convey to prospective employers.

~ *You want to subscribe to an electronic mail program, but don't know where to begin.* There are a wide range of electronic mail programs suitable for the novice to the experienced user with features varying from program to program, such as spelling check, attachments, file storage, and filtering. You'll need to evaluate which options and program best meet your needs and level of expertise.

~ *You plan to respond to an employment advertisement and no name is given.* Begin your message with "Dear Screening Committee" or "Dear Hiring Manager."

Formatting Electronic Letters

- Format the message for reading by separating your sentences into easy-to-read paragraphs.

Tip: Long paragraphs or no paragraphs are tough to read.

- Use paragraphs, spacing, and appropriate line width of no more than 70 characters to avoid text that runs together and premature line wraps.

Tip: If your message is too hard to read, a hiring manager won't bother.

Business Netiquette

Internet etiquette, known as netiquette, is an informal code of acceptable behavior for formal business communications on the Internet. While the Internet and electronic mail are less formal means of communication, people using this medium need to remain businesslike. Some rules to remember:

1. E-mail is public information, so always remember your correspondence may not be secure.
2. Capitalize appropriately when preparing your messages. Using all capitals is called shouting and is just as inappropriate as using all lowercase with no capitalization at all.
3. E-mail abbreviations have evolved for commonly written phrases, such as BTW for "by the way" or TIA for "thanks in advance." While these are acceptable in personal communications, they are not acceptable in business communications.
4. Don't use smiley faces or other alpha combinations that express emotions (sometimes referred to as emoticons) as they are not appropriate for business communications.

Electronic Letter Samples

Mr. Robinson:

Thank you for speaking with me on Thursday and discussing the systems analyst position. You answered many of my questions and I'm very interested in this opportunity.

I will make myself available for a personal meeting. Please let me know when this would be convenient.

Sincerely,

John Smith
(505) XXX-XXXX voice
Jsmith

Mr. Robinson:
Paul Jacobs at AAA Telecom suggested I contact you. I am currently a network engineer with a Fortune 1000 company and presently seeking a new challenge.

My qualifications include MCSE certification, ten years of experience as a systems administrator and network engineer, and an expertise in managing and administering LANs and WANs.

Communication is one of my strengths and I can easily explain all aspects of systems operations to both technical and lay personnel.

If you are aware of any opportunities, I would appreciate your contacting me at Johnmarley@abc.com.

Thanks for your help.

Sincerely,
John Marley
(212) XXX-XXXX Voice
JohnMarley@xyz.com

Dear Mr. Smith:

I am forwarding my résumé electronically in response to your recent ad in the Wall Street Journal.

My qualifications include three years of experience with an Internet start-up, researching, writing, editing, and managing production of a variety of text including Web site content, presentations, press releases, articles, videos, and speeches.

I have a Bachelor of Arts in Journalism and am highly skilled in working with diverse desktop publishing and presentation software.

I would be happy to discuss my credentials in further detail and look forward to hearing from you.

Sincerely,

Mary Mott
(910) XXX-XXXX voice
Mmott@xyz.com

Mr. Thomas:

Last evening I was researching career opportunities within the Twin Cities area that had an Internet/Intranet technology focus. I was pleasantly surprised to discover that such opportunities existed at ABC Company.

I have spent the last two years managing a $2.5-million Internet/Intranet technology initiative for my organization. We are in the final stages of implementation and will soon start to transition the project to our maintenance/support functions.

My current goal is a challenging opportunity that utilizes my knowledge base and skill set while allowing me to develop and advance to higher levels.

I sincerely believe that once you have reviewed my experience and qualifications, you will agree that my skills and experience can easily benefit your organization.

Thanking you in advance for your consideration. I look forward to speaking with you soon.

Sincerely,
Gayle Gold
(805) XXX-XXXX voice
Ggold@net.com

Responding to Advertisements

7

Advertisement responses are the most frequently prepared application letters. They are used by people to apply for jobs advertised in the newspaper employment listings and also to apply for other advertised positions, including on the Internet. Approximately 15 percent of all jobs are found through advertisements. Despite the low number, this job-lead source is used most often during the job search. As a result, advertisements generate thousands of responses. In other words, your letter will have lots of competition so your response must be written and formatted to catch attention.

How to Say It in Advertisement Responses

- STEP 1: With so much competition, craft an attention-grabbing introductory statement that captures the reader's interest.
- STEP 2: State the exact job title of the advertised position and identify where you saw the job listing.
- STEP 3: Customize each letter for a specific job opportunity and identify any special experiences, skills, interests, education, or training, whether included in your résumé or not, that shows why you would be the perfect candidate for the job.

Tip: Employers seek job candidates who meet their specific requirements, so it is vital that your response demonstrates clearly how your credentials match their needs.

- STEP 4: Include a reference in your letter that you have either enclosed or attached a copy of your résumé.
- STEP 5: Demonstrate your interest again in a closing statement.

in Advertisement Responses

- Do not include information, skills, education, or experience that have no relevance to the job opportunity. Extraneous information distracts the reader from what you have to offer.

- No matter how much you want or need the job, do not appear desperate; for example, beginning a letter with "Recently, I experienced a change in my career circumstances as a result of my company filing for Chapter 11, and eliminating 5,000 positions. Unfortunately, because of short tenure, I was among the casualties." This opening statement certainly grabs attention but it draws pity, not interest.

- Do not convey that you are just exploring opportunities and aren't sure whether the job is truly of interest. Employers want potential employees who are committed to job goals.

- Be focused and do not prepare untargeted letters that show you are interested in a variety of positions. Employers have specific needs and do not have time to play career counselor.

- Don't showcase generic skills, such as honesty, dependability, or motivation. Employers want to know how you meet their stated needs.

Tips on Writing Advertisement Responses

1. Review all potential job advertisement sources and cut out or print the listings or announcements you would like to pursue.

2. Read the job listing carefully and underscore the required and desired qualifications with a highlighting marker.

3. If the advertisement identifies the organization but doesn't provide an individual name, or requests that inquiries be sent to "Personnel Director," call and ask for a name (and spelling) so you can direct your letter more personally.

4. Begin with an opening statement indicating your interest in the position and where you located the opening, underscoring the titles of publications or using italics.

5. Use the body of the letter to illustrate how your experience, education, training, professional certifications, and skills parallel the advertised requirements. It is imperative that you address every specified qualification in the job listing.

6. If you have a special interest in an area of responsibility or plan to pursue additional training, state this information to bolster your credentials.

7. This type of letter is not followed up with a phone call, so your fourth paragraph should state only your availability and interest.

Tip: Special effects, such as bullets, can be used to focus attention on the mid-section of your letter where you outline your credentials.

Special Situations

 A job listing of interest gives a post office box with no mention of either the organization or contact name. Application letters need to be directed to specific individuals but, if you've been given no information, address the letter to "Dear Employer," a more contemporary option than "Sir," "Madam," or "Gentlemen."

 The listing does give a name but you can't tell whether the individual is a man or a woman. Use the full name in the salutation: "Dear Kelly Thomas."

 Some advertisements request a salary history or salary requirements. Recruiters I've discussed this with say they need this information in order to determine whether you fit into the job's salary range. However, you put yourself at a disadvantage in revealing what your requirements are without knowing the salary range. You must be aware, though, that if you don't include salary history or requirements when responding to an ad, you could exclude yourself from consideration. It's your decision. As a compromise, try and locate a recent occupational salary survey from a professional association, government agency, or executive recruiting firm. You can then state that your salary requirements are in line with the recent salary survey by XYZ organization.

~ *You find a job listing for the position of your dreams but, when you read the job requirements, you find you're not fully qualified.* This situation calls for a persuasive letter with a focus on the specified qualifications you do possess. Honestly state your passion for the position, industry, cause, or organization and how you will be able to make a contribution. Remember, nothing ventured, nothing gained. Employers can't always find a candidate with the exact credentials they seek.

~ *You've been mailing letters and getting no answers.* Try to get an edge on the competition by mailing your responses on Sunday or Monday. If that doesn't give you enough time to craft well-written letters, don't rush the process; mail the letters later in the week. Hiring managers differ on letter timing. When they're under pressure to fill jobs, they like them in by Tuesday to make the first interview cut. If a closing date is listed, most wait until that date to review all letters and résumés. One manager believes he gets better letters later in the week; possibly the letters reflect the time taken to research and prepare.

Words to Use in Advertisement Responses

ability	attached	certification
accomplishments	background	confident
advertisement	benefit	credentials
announcement	candidate	current

demonstrated	include	qualifications
discuss	interest	qualifies
diversified	match	similarity
enclosed	opportunities	skills
experience	parallel	strengths
expertise	possibilities	unique
highlights	posting	viable
identical		

Phrases to Use in Advertisement Responses

as outlined in the enclosed résumé

asset to your management team

available to meet with you

closely match

consider my record of accomplishment

delighted to see your advertisement

discuss how I can help

discuss my qualifications and your needs

eager to work with your management team

excited about the possibility

experience matches your requirements

favorable consideration

highlights of my achievements

in my current position

interested in this position

like to meet with you and discuss

look forward to our meeting

makes me a viable candidate

meet with you in person

most recently these skills

my qualifications include

my strongest assets

new challenge

of particular interest

quickly establish myself

solid background in

strong interest in

the following accomplishments highlight

thoroughly experienced in all phases

well suited

will be relocating

would appreciate the opportunity

would like to put my experience and skills to use

your requirements

Sentences to Use in Advertisement Responses

As outlined in the enclosed résumé, I have seven years' experience establishing and implementing credit and collection programs and maintaining cash flows for $55 million in annual revenue.

I am eager to learn more about the nursing supervisor position and would like to discuss my qualifications and interests with you.

I can contribute to your organization's effectiveness by establishing good working relations with customers and personnel at all organizational levels.

I look forward to speaking with you.

I would like to put my experience and skills to use as the Human Resources Manager you advertised for in the May 5, 20XX *Washington Post*.

If you are looking for a candidate with exceptional editing skills and a commitment to excellence, please call me to schedule a meeting.

My extensive horticulture and landscape design experience qualifies me for the Landscape Supervisor position advertised in Sunday's *Chicago Tribune*.

My previous experience incorporates handling all accounting functions within the finance division.

My qualifications and diversified background include both hands-on and management experience with large-scale laundry operations in full-service and convention hotels.

Thank you for your time and consideration.

With more than ten years' experience in the customer service field, my experience matches your requirements for a Customer Service Manager.

Your organization impresses me by the performance of your products and the integrity of your support staff.

Your recent advertisement for an Environmental Engineer in Sunday's *Democrat & Chronicle* is an exact match for my qualifications.

Paragraphs to Use in Advertisement Responses

Five years of marketing experience in the automotive industry have earned me the reputation of a high performer who achieves optimal results. My employers have rewarded me with rapid promotions and increased responsibilities.

I am eager to learn more about the Java Programmer position and would like to discuss my qualifications and interests with you. Thanks for your time and consideration.

I am interested in the position and would appreciate the opportunity to discuss my background and your requirements in greater detail. I look forward to hearing from you.

Last year, under my direction, my organization achieved the highest regional award for sales support. The enclosed résumé outlines my experience and contributions.

My career goal is to use my industrial design expertise in a corporate setting. I would welcome the opportunity to discuss how I can make a contribution at CCB. I will call you to set up an appointment.

My expertise is in the initiation and implementation of customer care programs. I have recently successfully integrated sales and customer service support for a multinational corporation.

My qualifications are ideal for the Health Services Coordinator position you advertised through National Association of Health Care Administrators. My six years of provider relations experience with an HMO/PPO matches your stated preferences.

The attached résumé outlines my education and experience. I would like to meet with you to explore employment opportunities with AXX Company. I can be reached at (XXX) XXX-XXXX.

The enclosed résumé summarizes my experience and demonstrates my progressive advancement in the telecommunications industry. It's time for me to make a change and I'd like to explore the project management opportunities with ABC company.

The teaching position described in *Teacher's Journal* sounds exactly like the opportunity I am seeking. I would like to use my skills to motivate your students to reach their potential.

Thanks for your attention. I look forward to speaking with you.

Sample Advertisement Responses

Here are eight sample advertisement responses. The sources include a Web site and a newspaper.

GEORGE MAXWELL

99 Lavender Lane
Old Westbury, New York 11560
Work (212) XXX-XXXX Home (516) XXX-XXXX

September 4, 20XX

Guardi Pharmaceuticals
Albert Tuccillo, Sales Director
35 Park Avenue
New York, NY 20000

Dear Albert:

I would like the opportunity to put my energy, drive, and enthusiasm to work as the New York City Sales Manager advertised for on our corporate Web site. A solid pharmaceutical sales background, superior product knowledge, and excellent interpersonal skills make me confident I would be a productive addition to your staff.

My qualifications, as detailed in the enclosed résumé, include:

- Over 12 years of award-winning sales performance with Guardi Pharmaceuticals, culminating with the "Senior Professional Award" in 1999.

- Exceptional communication skills, connecting easily with customers and Guardi personnel, forging and building effective professional relationships.

My managers have consistently praised my ability to achieve results, regardless of assignment.

I am a quick learner and interested in taking on new challenges while capitalizing on my strengths in establishing relationships and partnerships.

I would like to be part of your team and look forward to a personal meeting.

Sincerely,

George Maxwell

Enclosure

HILLARY GAMBEL
41 Fifteenth Street
Longwood, Florida 32700
(305) XXX-XXXX

July 1, 20XX

Sunnyside Management Group
15 Ocean Boulevard
Tampa, FL 33600

Dear Director of Human Resources:

Your advertisement for a Property Manager in Sunday's *Tampa Tribune* excited me. I'd like to work with your management team in making this newly renovated property a success!

My qualifications and diversified background include both hands-on and management experience with front office and housekeeping operations. The following accomplishments highlight some of my strengths and abilities:

- Consistently meet/exceed the needs and requirements of guests. Perform beyond job expectations to satisfy guest needs.
- Adeptly utilize computer registration system; train new employees on computerized system and customer relations.
- Effectively and efficiently resolve guest inquiries and complaints.
- Piloted an employment satisfaction survey. Spearheaded initiatives and procedures that reduced employee turnover and improved morale.

I'd like to meet with you in person to further discuss my qualifications and your needs.

Sincerely yours,

Hillary Gambel

Encl.

DOUGLAS MANCHESTER, CPA

8900 Eagle Circle
Saint Louis, Missouri 63119
(314) XXX-XXXX

April 12, 20XX

Harper & Harper
Abigail Tree
Staffing Manager
88 Seventh Avenue
Saint Louis, MO 63110

Dear Ms. Tree:

I was delighted when I saw your advertisement for an Accountant in the April 9th *Post Dispatch*. I was struck by the similarities in your requirements and my accounting background.

The enclosed résumé highlights my qualifications and achievements:

- Five years of experience with a CPA firm
- Masters of Science in Accounting
- Certified Public Accountant
- Expertise in using automated accounting systems

As a tax accountant for a large, local real estate developer, I miss the challenge, intensity, and variety I experienced in public accounting.

The combination of my technical ability, experience, and hardworking nature makes me a viable candidate. I look forward to hearing from you and scheduling an appointment to discuss employment opportunities at Harper & Harper.

Sincerely,

Douglas Manchester, CPA

Encl.

MARIA SANTIAGO

65 Greyhound Street
Coral Gables, Florida 33133
(305) XXX-XXXX

July 5, 20XX

CABLE USA
H. Wilson
45 Fourth Avenue
New York, NY 10021

Dear H. Wilson:

Your advertisement from *Television Media Journal* for a Television Reporter—Spanish Language is an exact match for my qualifications. My five years' experience as a television reporter for WXKZ Miami, a Spanish language station, parallels your advertised requirements.

Your Needs	My Qualifications
1. U.S. Citizen.	1. Naturalized U.S. Citizen.
2. Strong journalistic skills.	2. Extensive experience researching, gathering information, preparing stories, and presenting facts clearly and succinctly. Nominated for an Emmy award for "Health Care Scam," a medical fraud report.
3. Professional broadcast voice as evidenced by native fluency.	3. Native fluency in English and Spanish. Pleasant, well-controlled voice with good timing. Excellent pronunciation.
4. Excellent translation/adaptation abilities with fluency in both English and Spanish.	4. Raised in a bilingual household. Dual Spanish/English major in college. Correct English and Spanish usage.

I am interested in the challenge this position presents and would like to meet with you and share my enthusiasm and commitment to support the Spanish-speaking community. I have enclosed writing/translation examples and a sample video tape.

Sincerely,

Maria Santiago

Enclosures (3)

Josephine A. Parker
7553 Broadway, Houston, Texas 77050
(713) XXX-XXXX

February 5, 20XX

Wildlife Preservation
Dean Jones
P.O. Box 12
The Woodlands, TX 77380

Dear Mr. Jones:

The advertisement in your newsletter for an Administrative Assistant to the Communications Manager intrigued me. I did some research and discovered Wildlife Preservation offers growth, challenge, and teamwork, the very things I'm looking for in an organization. Your mission in preservation added to my excitement and desire to be a member of your organization.

My seven years of secretarial and administrative experience qualify me for the position. I possess excellent communication skills, the ability to work well with all staff levels, set priorities, and follow through assignments to completion. In addition, I hold a life-long commitment to preservation.

Nature has played an integral part in my life since childhood and has kindled a passionate fascination in plants and wildlife. My interest in your organization was piqued by your articles on Big Thicket Natural Preserve and Alabama-Coushatta Indian Reservation. During residence in Beaumont, I had the opportunity to navigate the Village Creek and experience the fauna and flora.

I want to be part of your team at Wildlife Preservation and aid in safeguarding our nation's biological heritage. I look forward to speaking with you and exploring your needs and my qualifications in more detail.

Sincerely yours,

Josephine A. Parker

Enclosure

THOMAS O'BRIEN

574 Third Avenue, Culver City, California 90230

(310) XXX-XXXX

October 3, 20XX

Western Manufacturers
44 First Street
Los Angeles, CA 90012

Dear Employer:

My extensive experience in contract administration makes me highly qualified for the Senior Contracts Administrator position you advertised in the October 3, 20XX *Los Angeles Times*.

Ten years of financial experience in the high tech industry earned me the reputation of a dedicated team player who gets the job done. My efforts have been rewarded with increased responsibility.

My credentials include:

- Master's in Business Administration
- Six years' experience in budget preparation and financial analysis
- Four years' experience in contract administration
- Expertise in proposal preparation and negotiation
- Hands-on experience with Microsoft Excel, Word, and other software programs
- Working knowledge of FAR and DAR

Throughout my career, my supervisors have consistently recognized my personal commitment and ability to meet all assigned objectives.

The enclosed résumé outlines my education and experience. I would like to meet with you to explore employment opportunities with your company. I can be reached at (310) XXX-XXXX and look forward to hearing from you.

Sincerely,

Thomas O'Brien

Enclosure

FRANK FRENCH
45 Columbia Court, Trenton, NJ 08068
(609) XXX-XXXX

June 3, 20XX

Cutting Edge Computers, Inc.
Attn: Mr. Wilbur Jeffries
Human Resources Manager
99 Main Street
Newark, NJ 07854

Dear Mr. Jeffries:

Your advertisement in the June 1, 20XX *Star-Ledger* for a Computer Sales Representative describes exactly the position I am seeking.

My four years of sales experience qualifies me for this position. I am highly skilled in identifying revenue opportunities, prioritizing accounts, and developing action plans.

I consistently achieved 120% to 175% of sales objectives by persevering, overcoming objections, and persistently closing sales.

While my experience has been in the telecommunications industry, I have had a long-term interest in computers and would like the opportunity to transfer my solid sales skills while diligently learning the computer industry.

It's impossible to convey my interest, enthusiasm, and positive spirit on paper. I'd like the opportunity to meet with you and demonstrate my desire and ability to take on this challenging position.

I look forward to hearing from you.

Sincerely,

Frank French

Encl.

MAURA O'RILEY

1244 North 23rd Street, Arlington, Virginia 22204 (703) XXX-XXXX

May 10, 20XX

National Association of Certified Pharmacists
Mr. Tom Jones, Executive Search Chair
2455 Pennsylvania Avenue
Washington, D.C. 20001

Dear Mr. Jones:

A desire for professional growth sparked my interest in the Executive Director position advertised on your Web site.

As a resourceful manager with progressive experience and consistent top performance, I am presently Executive Director of a national association. I manage all association operations while promoting and providing annual nationwide competency testing of over 6,000 candidates.

Currently, I work effectively with the Board of Directors, setting agendas for board meetings and preparing annual budgets of $4.6 million. In addition, I oversee development and approval of continuing education and liaison with licensing boards.

My accomplishments include:
- Increasing exam registrations by 141%
- Enhancing association image from an individual and national perspective
- Improving procedures that increased association renewal rates
- Designing grant procedures and achieving more effective fund disbursements

My education and credentials include:
- Master of Science in Public Administration
- Certified Association Executive (CAE), the American Society of Association Executives

The enclosed résumé outlines my qualifications. I am confident I can be a valuable addition to your association. I would like to meet with you and discuss how I can assist the National Association of Certified Pharmacists in reaching its goals.

Sincerely,

Maura O'Riley

Enclosure

Sending Unsolicited Letters $\boxed{8}$

The happiest employees are those who find organizations that are in sync with their personalities and values. Why not do some research to identify organizations you'd like to work for and send an unsolicited letter, presenting yourself as a potential employee? The unsolicited letter or self-directed approach has an added benefit: There's less competition when you're not applying with the pack.

Tips on Researching Potential Employers

What type of organization do you want to work for? Large or small? For profit or nonprofit? Privately or publicly owned? If in the public sector, do you want to work for the federal, state, or local government? Even when the type of position you are seeking is available in all types of organizations, the jobs may be different because the structure and personality of the organizations differ.

Tip: Consider organizations that produce products or services that you find handy or useful. Ask friends and contacts about likely prospects.

A self-directed approach gives you great flexibility in choosing organizations that meet your needs and values. Put your investigative skills to use in tracking down likely candidates, developing a list of employment possibilities including names, addresses, phone numbers, and senior staff members. Read everything you can about companies and their leaders utilizing:

- the Internet
- articles in business and trade magazines, journals, newsletters, and local and national newspapers

Tip: Use these sources for identifying senior staff, understanding an organization's philosophy and mission, and learning about its services and products.

- local business calendars
- Yellow Pages of the phone directory
- local directories of business and industry

Tip: Keep an eye open for news of recent moves, mergers, acquisitions, contract awards, and who's moving where. Use the research techniques you will find in Chapter 15.

in Unsolicited Letters

- STEP 1: Once you find an organization that interests you, do additional research to identify the appropriate hiring manager, either through the organization's Web site, the Internet, directories, networking, or calling the organization directly. Confirm the correct spelling of the individual's name and his or her exact job title.
- STEP 2: Employers get lots of unsolicited mail, most of which ends up in the wastepaper basket. To make sure your letter is read, write a catchy opening and create an appealing format.
- STEP 3: Write a short paragraph that summarizes your experience and accomplishments, quickly demonstrating what you have to offer.
- STEP 4: Prepare a paragraph that details your most recent position. Share with the employer the breadth and scope of your experience, responsibility, and achievements.

- STEP 5: End your letter on a positive note by stating your interest in meeting with them. Always indicate that you will call them to schedule an appointment.

Tip: You'll make the letter more personal if you repeat the employer's name in the last paragraph. For example: "Mr. Jones, I will call you within the next five days to schedule an appointment."

---

in Unsolicited Letters

- Negative statements such as "I realize my background may not be congruent with your current needs."
- Self-serving statements; for example, "The objective of this letter is to request your assistance and any possible suggestions you might have in my pursuit of a new position."
- Vague statements like "In the event that there may be a mutually beneficial position open, I have enclosed a copy of my résumé."
- Any requests that the recipients refer you to someone else if they don't have an opening. Most people don't go to bat for someone they don't know.
- Closing statements that provide your phone number, inferring the recipient should be the one to take the initiative and call you.

Tips on Writing Unsolicited Letters

1. Take a creative approach in crafting your first paragraph. Read business magazines and business sections in newspapers and on the Internet to locate information about the economy, industry, or the organization. Use this to personalize your initial paragraph and to show the employer that you're in tune with your occupation and the business/industry environment.

2. Avoid the human resources department by addressing the letter to the highest level manager in the division your position falls under. This will increase the odds of your letter winding up with the hiring manager, the individual most likely to make the hiring decision.

3. Be very specific in your letter. Clearly show how your experience, skills, credentials, and accomplishments would be an asset to this employer.

4. Let your unique personality come through; it will spark greater interest in your letter.

5. Show your enthusiasm for the job, organization, industry, or location.

6. Use a positive, assertive tone in your close. State that you will call them—and make sure you do. Hiring managers tell me all the time that they put such letters in a pile to retrieve when you do call. They claim very few people actually follow up their letters with a phone call.

Special Situations

    ❧ *You're not sure what you have to offer.* You'll need to do some occupational and industry research to see where you fit in. Prepare to network and use informational interviews to define your job objective and discover realistically for what positions you are suited. Letters that imply the reader should figure out where you would best fit into an organization are usually tossed out. Employers are not interested in playing career counselor.

    ❧ *You're planning to relocate.* The unsolicited letter is perfect to use in this situation. Scout out potential employers and positions in the new location by researching through the Internet, subscribing to local newspapers, and accessing telephone books at the local library. Then, follow the steps in How to Say It . . . on page 152.

    ❧ *The organization of interest has several divisions.* Either send a letter to one division and, if you come up empty-handed, send a letter to another division. Or, send letters to all the targeted individuals at each division.

Words to Use in Unsolicited Letters

accomplishments	growth	profitability
appointment	interest	recognized
arrange	interview	relocating
asset	introduce	research
benefit	looking	review
call	meet	seasoned
contribute	meeting	seeking
experience	organization	services
firm	productivity	utilize

Phrases to Use in Unsolicited Letters

are you seeking

could you use

during my five years

for the past two years

I plan to relocate

I would welcome a meeting

If your organization

I'm available to meet

In my present position

It's extremely difficult

most recently

my experience and accomplishments qualify me

my expertise in

my financial management qualifications include

the enclosed résumé provides

will call you

Sentences to Use in Unsolicited Letters

Are you looking for broad in-depth computer and instructional experience in a senior-level professional?

As a results-oriented team player, I have successfully managed multiple projects simultaneously for changing human resources and business environments in diverse industries.

As a senior executive with a leading consulting firm, I direct a 200-member information systems organization that creates information technology strategies enabling businesses to compete globally.

During the week of June 10 I will be visiting in the New York area and would like to speak with you concerning opportunities with NBC.

I currently direct an organization that meets unique client needs by customizing training services that improve delivery of quality initiatives.

I will call you within five days to schedule an appointment.

I would like to meet with you personally to discuss how I can contribute to the project's success.

If you are interested in a Marketing Manager with a proven track record, let's meet and discuss how I can utilize my skills to meet Ritten Corporation's needs.

If you are looking for a performer with strong technical skills and a willingness to work hard to get the job done, please contact me to schedule a meeting.

If your hospital would benefit from a dynamic, motivated nursing professional with a management background in health care delivery systems, then you will find my qualifications interesting.

It is increasingly difficult to find qualified individuals to install and maintain cable systems.

Let me increase your employees' productivity by designing and delivering training seminars that build teams and promote a cooperative work environment.

Recent articles in *Fast Company* magazine highlight your organization as one of the fastest growing online insurance providers.

While my abilities and training are a plus, I am also a dedicated performer who doesn't mind starting at the ground floor and working my way up.

Paragraphs to Use in Unsolicited Letters

A life-long interest in skin care products and the role they play in appearance and well-being will enhance my ability to successfully market Horizon. I would like to be part of the team launching the sale of this wonderful product.

Career growth and challenge are my goals. If you are looking for a seasoned insurance professional, I would welcome the opportunity to focus my energies on making a valuable contribution to XYZ Insurance Corporation.

I am confident I will be a valuable addition to your accounting firm. I would like to meet with you and discuss how I can help Blooms and Finer meet its goals.

I have a lot to offer as an Executive Assistant. I am committed to high standards and goals and would like to meet with you in person to discuss them.

My family claims I was born with a green thumb! An early interest in plants nurtured a desire to pursue a career in horticulture.

Ms. Linden, I am interested in meeting with you and discussing opportunities at National Telecomm. I'll give you a call next week to schedule an appointment.

The enclosed résumé can't reveal the many details that make the difference between a so-so employee and one who contributes daily. I am ready to meet with you personally to determine if a match exists and then discuss employment possibilities.

Sample Unsolicited Letters

The following ten samples will help you write unsolicited letters.

SANDY SPRINGFELLOW
855 Windy Court
Darien, Connecticut 06824
(213) XXX-XXXX

March 1, 20XX

National Industries
Sharon Hammer
Vice President, Administration
58 Duke Lane
Darien, CT 06820

Dear Ms. Hammer:

Customers influence business outcomes. Satisfied customers generate repeat sales, new business, and make the difference between profit and loss.

I can help your organization satisfy your customers by working effectively with marketing, service, and administrative groups to ensure optimal customer support.

As a highly motivated, detail-oriented Customer Service Supervisor, I have developed excellent skills in written and oral communications, problem solving, and follow-up.

My recent performance evaluation states:

"Customer satisfaction is at an all-time high. Exceptional performance by Sandy deserves credit in excellent training, management, and follow-up of her people. Very quick to identify problem areas and takes good corrective measures to resolve them quickly."

I would like the opportunity to satisfy National Industries' customers and assist your organization in reaching its goals. When would it be convenient for us to meet?

Sincerely,

Sandy Springfellow

Encl.

655 Fairview Lane
Cincinnati, Ohio 45222

Contact: Stephen W. Mueller
(513) XXX-XXXX

FOR IMMEDIATE RELEASE

MARKETING SPECIALIST SEEKS NEW OPPORTUNITY

Are you in need of a talented professional to write and produce promotional materials, including direct mail, press releases, product sheets, and other marketing and sales support materials?

Stephen W. Mueller offers ten years' experience writing and producing marketing and sales materials that get results. His excellent interpersonal and communication skills have enabled him to work effectively with Product, Sales, and Marketing Managers, identifying and interpreting their promotional needs.

Expertise and accomplishments:

- Ability to plan, coordinate, and produce news releases, printed materials, and advertising for an international leader in electronic publishing and CD-ROM
- Experience in developing booth materials and producing slides and product announcements for national and international trade shows and related workshops
- Desktop publishing skills using Pagemaker and Quark Express
- Bachelor of Science in Marketing

Stephen is presently employed, but he is available for interviews. For further information, call (513) XXX-XXXX.

# # #

GAYLE L. SLOAN
77 Main Street, Los Angeles, California 90012
Work (310) XXX-XXXX Home (310) XXX-XXXX

August 2, 20XX

XCEL Incorporated
Philip Mariner
Vice President, Administration
3 Palm Court
Los Angeles, CA 90012

Dear Mr. Mariner:

If your organization would benefit from a dynamic and motivated curriculum specialist with technical ability, then you will find my qualifications interesting.

Highlights of my experience include:

- Five years of experience designing curriculum for end-user training on system applications.
- Proficient in using PowerPoint and word-processing software to write and produce workbooks, visual aids, test cases, and course materials.
- Development of a new system user manual appropriate for all skill levels.
- Installation of systems at satellite locations and long-term user support.

The enclosed résumé provides more detailed information on my background. I would like the opportunity to meet with you in person to discuss your needs and how I can meet them. I will call you next week to set up an appointment.

Sincerely yours,

Gayle L. Sloan

Enclosure

JAMES COUGHLIN
33 Bayside Lane, Boston, Massachusetts 02110
(617) XXX-XXXX

October 1, 20XX

Zycom Telecommunications
Suzanne Price, CEO
One Elden Street
Herndon, VA 20170

Dear Ms. Price:

As organizations strive to improve profitability and productivity while maintaining a competitive edge, there is a growing need for senior executives who can manage change and transition while strengthening the bottom line.

As a results-oriented leader, I have successfully directed telecommunications companies through a dynamic and turbulent business environment.

The following accomplishments, detailed in the enclosed résumé, highlight some of my strengths and abilities:

- Doubled annual sales revenue through the development and implementation of leading-edge services.
- Established innovative marketing programs including reseller, agent, and telemarketing.
- Devised successful marketing programs to target, penetrate, and acquire new business.

I am seeking a new challenge and am interested in relocating to the Northern Virginia area. I will be in Herndon the week of November 1 and would like to speak with you to discuss opportunities with your organization. I will call to set up an appointment.

Sincerely yours,

James Coughlin

Enclosure

KYLE WATERMAN

90 Liberty Lane
Philadelphia, Pennsylvania 19120
(215) XXX-XXXX

February 14, 20XX

Metropolitan Printers
Zachary Wells, General Manager
97 Dominion Drive
Philadelphia, PA 19100

Dear Mr. Wells:

Could your organization use a graphic designer and illustrator who thrives in a fast-paced, demanding environment while producing creative, high-quality products?

My background includes over five years of experience in desktop publishing and design. My strengths are my drawing ability, keen graphic sense, and a natural aptitude for design composition. I use effective communication skills to make highly technical information and ideas understandable to targeted audiences.

My employer has consistently praised the high quality of my products. The attached résumé and samples reflect the level and variety of my capabilities.

I would like to meet with you in person and discuss becoming a part of your team. I will call you to schedule an appointment.

Thank you for your time and consideration.

Sincerely,

Kyle Waterman

Enclosures (4)

WILLIAM WASHINGTON
72 Chester Lane, Huntsville, Alabama 35800
(205) XXX-XXXX (Work) (205) XXX-XXXX (Home)

January 1, 20XX

BBB Corporation
Ms. Jane Doe
Vice President/Controller
6 First Avenue
Huntsville, AL 35805

Dear Ms. Doe:

Do you believe that leading, motivating, and training employees promotes enthusiasm, makes the workplace more enjoyable, and invigorates the bottom line? If so, we have a lot in common and should explore developing a relationship.

In my five years of administrative experience in a technical environment, I have developed skills in budget and financial reporting practices, overseeing performance review programs, and supervising staffing needs, requirements, and assignments. I have excellent interpersonal and communication skills and can quickly develop rapport at all staff levels.

Most recently, I directed facility modifications and coordinated two office moves—efficiently, effectively, and on time.

Ms. Doe, I would like to discuss with you how I can apply my administrative expertise to an Assistant Division Administrator position with BBB Corporation. I will call you to set up an appointment.

I look forward to speaking with you.

Sincerely,

William Washington

Enclosure

NELLIE STEVENS

88 Landing Court, Buffalo, New York 14200
(716) XXX-XXXX

June 4, 20XX

Victoria Square
Mr. Kirk Jeffries
Human Resources Director
8000 Signal Drive
Buffalo, NY 14220

Dear Mr. Jeffries:

Can you use a skilled fashion professional with a flair for transforming merchandise into fashion excitement? If so, consider me for a Display Manager position with Victoria Square.

My qualifications, as outlined in the enclosed résumé, include:

- Six years' experience stimulating and increasing sales by creating captivating window and department displays.
- Proven record in promoting merchandise and products through innovative themes and staging.
- Talent for coordinating individual pieces into unique combinations and ensembles.
- Bachelor of Arts in Fashion Merchandising from Fashion Institute of Technology.

I am ready for a new challenge and would like to meet with you to demonstrate my commitment and desire to make a contribution to Victoria Square. I will call you to set up a personal meeting.

Thank you for your consideration.

Sincerely yours,

Nellie Stevens

Enclosure

JAQUELINE PARK

79 Church Street, Eau Claire, Wisconsin 54700 (715) XXX-XXXX

November 17, 20XX

National Brands
Mr. Hood
Director of Training
28 Bishop Road
Eau Claire, WI 54700

Dear Mr. Hood:

Are your employees using their computer software effectively? According to a new study conducted by Users.com, 76% of all employees learn only the basics of software applications.

Let me increase your employees' productivity by designing and conducting training programs for groups and individuals that promote efficient use of existing software.

For the past five years, I have worked for a computer training center where I established and coordinated a computer lab and developed software courses and curricula that satisfied student needs.

My expertise in computer applications resulted in my designation as "PC Expert" for the entire training center. Now I would like to put my experience and skills to use at National Brands as a technical trainer.

The enclosed résumé provides more information on my background. I'd like to meet with you personally to discuss your organizational needs. I will call you to set up an appointment.

Thank you for your time.

Yours truly,

Jaqueline Park

Encl.

NEIL GREEN
55 Hunters Way, New Orleans, Louisiana 70100
(504) XXX-XXXX

February 15, 20XX

Communication One
Mr. Beam, Service Manager
544 Telecom Way
New Orleans, LA 70110

Dear Mr. Beam:

It is increasingly difficult to find qualified individuals to install and maintain cable systems.

During my ten years in the telecommunications industry, I have developed a specialty in large cable designs. My qualifications include:

- Technical expertise and the unique ability to find innovative solutions.
- Quick and accurate engineering and cost estimates at less than a 1% installed cost variance.
- Consistent record in identifying and surpassing customer requirements resulting in satisfied customers and a quality reputation.

In my present position, I supervise subcontractor cable projects from 100 to 3,000 lines, estimating material costs and providing building, plant, and campus cable engineering and layout. Additional qualifications are highlighted in the enclosed résumé.

Mr. Beam, I'm interested in meeting with you and discussing opportunities at Communication One. I'll give you a call next week to schedule an appointment.

Thank you for your time.

Sincerely,

Neil Green

Enclosure

Russell Martin

9 Cactus Court, Phoenix, Arizona 85014 (602) XXX-XXXX

February 20, 20XX

Golden Development Company
Steve Preston, President
Mountain Way
Colorado Springs, CO 80903

Dear Mr. Preston:

If your organization could benefit from creating new business opportunities and improving/expanding existing operations, then you will find my qualifications to be of interest.

As a Senior Executive with extensive management experience in design, construction, and operations, I am a recognized specialist in delivering large, complex commercial development programs on time and within budget.

My qualifications, detailed in the enclosed résumé, are strongest in providing a full range of development-related services for small- to super-regional-size projects, including site planning, engineering, design, construction, and tenant administration. I also contribute expertise and recommendations from land acquisition and predevelopment through design, construction, and property management support.

I currently direct an organization that meets unique client needs by customizing services in project analysis, design management, construction consulting, and tenant coordination for offices, shopping centers, and department stores.

I am interested in taking on a new challenge and would like to discuss opportunities with your organization. I will be in Colorado Springs the week of March 3 and will call you to set up an appointment.

Thank you for your time.

Sincerely,

Russell Martin

Encl.

Getting a Little Help from a Friend— Networking and Referral Letters

9

You're probably familiar with the expression, "It's not what you know, but whom you know." Making contact with others expands your job search options and enables you to access resources and people when you need them.

The ways to connect are limited only by your imagination. It's possible to access people and information through professional and trade associations, unions, groups, networks, the Internet, conferences, meetings, workshops, speeches, classes, and lectures. View every personal exchange as a link to information and resources.

A network of contacts is your best and most effective tool for achieving your job search and career goals. It is the most productive source for information on job and career opportunities.

Networks are a wonderful source for referrals. The hiring process is time-consuming and risky, and referrals minimize the risk for recruiters. If a recruiter or hiring manager knows and is comfortable with the work and values of the person referring you, chances are he or she will assume you have similar work ethics and values. Referrals are so prized that many organizations offer a bonus to employees for referring desirable candidates.

 in Referral Letters

- STEP 1: Begin with an opening paragraph that indicates how you located the contact. Did you hear them speak? Did they author an article or publication? Did you read about them on the Internet? Were they quoted in an article? If referred, identify the individual who recommended that you write. The recipient should personally know this individual and be able to quickly make a connection.

- STEP 2: Introduce yourself in the second paragraph, detailing the information or help you are seeking or why you are interested in the organization or position.

- STEP 3: Follow this paragraph with a descriptive summary or short paragraphs that showcase your experience and accomplishments that would be of interest to the organization or fulfill their job requirements.

- STEP 4: Include a statement that demonstrates how you are uniquely qualified.

- STEP 5: Close on a positive note indicating either your desire to speak with them or learn more about the organization or position.

Tip: Provide a telephone number or electronic mail address where you can be reached.

- STEP 6: End your letter by thanking them for their help.

 ## in Referral Letters

- Avoid putting the contact on the defensive by asking for a job.
- Don't expect the contact to play career counselor and help you choose a career direction.
- Refrain from making demands.
- Don't confuse networking as a substitute for a placement agency. Have realistic expectations.
- Avoid asking for too much; refine and target your requests.
- Don't make multiple requests; one at a time is appropriate.

Tips on Writing Referral Letters

1. Try to locate members of your network who know the individuals who can help you and let the referral pave the way.
2. Be specific in your request. Are you looking for referral sources, industry information, hiring organizations, or job opportunities?
3. Plan what you are requesting.
4. Ask for advice, not a job.
5. Don't misspell the name of either the person who has referred you or the referral.
6. Avoid any statements or expressions that make you appear aggressive, overly confident, or too eager.

Tip: Strive for a humble tone.

---

7. Refrain from alluding to a special relationship with a key member within the organization, especially if he or she is a relative.
8. Beyond the initial paragraph, referral letters are similar to the unsolicited letter. You can often save an unsolicited letter as a new document, craft a different introductory paragraph, and then modify the content slightly for your targeted recipient.

Special Situations

～ *You don't know anyone who can provide a referral.* Even if you have never actively networked, you already have an established network of contacts to generate referrals. It is just a matter of identifying and tapping into it. Your network consists of:

—Your family: your spouse, parents, siblings, aunts, uncles, cousins, other relatives, and their networks

—Your friends, neighbors, former neighbors, and their networks

—Your former classmates and their parents, teachers, guidance and career counselors, alumni, fraternity and sorority members, and their networks

—Your present and former employers and colleagues, supervisors, subordinates, customers, clients, suppliers, competitors, and their networks

—Your present and former professional, civic, and trade association and union members, board of directors, staff, and their networks

—Your lawyer, accountant, doctor, dentist, clergy, insurance agent, banker, and their networks

—Your plumber, painter, electrician, hairdresser, dry cleaner, other service workers, and their networks

—The store owners and salespeople in the stores you frequent, and their networks

—Any clubs, club members, and enthusiasts who share your personal interests and hobbies, and their networks

~ *You don't know anyone to contact.* Start by talking to people you know and ask them if they know of anyone who can help you identify opportunities in your field. When you contact these individuals, ask if they know anyone else who may help you. Networking is a multiplication game; you'll develop and build on your contacts and personal referrals to make more contacts and learn of more job opportunities. The more contacts you make, the greater your chances of locating a job by networking.

~ *You would like to change industries and all your contacts are in another industry.* Tell every person you know that you are looking for a job in a specific industry. Tell friends, family, someone who works at an organization you would like to work for, or has a thread of a connection. Try to get the person you know to act as a referral or introduction.

~ *You don't want to ask for favors.* Many people feel uncomfortable soliciting help, but you'll expedite your search if you do. Most individuals in your network are happy to lend their support and expertise; just remember to make only one request from each contact.

~ *You are unsure of the correct spelling of your referral.* Call your contact back, apologize, and verify the spelling. Or, contact the organization directly and ask the receptionist or a human resources staff member for the correct spelling.

~ *You don't know the person who made the referral personally.* As long as the person suggested you contact this individual, it is fine to use the person's name.

Words to Use in Referral Letters

accomplishments	expertise	opening
achievements	exploring	opportunities
acquaintance	feels	outlined
advice	fill	position
appointment	friend	pursue
appreciate	goals	read
assets	heard	recommended
assistance	highlights	referred
aware	ideas	researching
believes	indicated	résumé
career	industry	schedule
change	informed	seeking
compatible	interest	spoken
contact	job	strongest
convenience	know	suggested
employment	looking	support
enclosed	meet	thoughts
expansion	mentioned	transition
experience	mutual	vacancy

Phrases to Use in Referral Letters

a mutual acquaintance

aware of event management opportunities

could we schedule

Donna Roth indicated

enjoyed your training program

exploring the financial planning industry

get your input

hear your suggestions

heard you speak

I would appreciate

informed me of the opening

interested in meeting

John Murray suggested

member of Toastmasters

my sister, Kathleen Little, Billing Manager at XYZ

our mutual friend

plan to transition

pleasure to meet you

recommended I contact

referred me to you

seeking an IT position

spoke highly

suggested I contact you

thought my experience is compatible

Sentences to Use in Referral Letters

Barbara Thomas indicated you would have a vacancy in the finance department within the next four weeks.

Harry Smith suggested I contact you concerning the opening in your engineering department.

I am interested in entering the training and development field and would appreciate any suggestions you could offer.

I am seeking advice concerning my next career move.

I could use your help.

I would appreciate your advice and ideas.

It was wonderful to finally meet you at the International Banking Conference.

Lester Williams of your Boston office mentioned that you had an opening for an experienced LAN administrator.

Malcolm Wilson informed me of your impending expansion into e-commerce.

My goal is not to find a job but to explore opportunities within the transportation industry.

The project excites me, and I would like to be a part of your team.

Your expertise will help me gain insight into the securities market in New York City.

Your help is greatly appreciated.

Your firm interests me, and I have kept abreast of its activities through industry contacts, recent articles, and a campus presentation made by Bruce Jones and Julia Brill of your Detroit office.

Paragraphs to Use in Referral Letters

A mutual friend, Pamela Jones, shared your recruitment plans to expand the sales team. I am currently looking for a career opportunity that will utilize my sales expertise and would like to meet with you to discuss your expansion goals.

Congratulations on your appointment as President of Nature Conservancy. I am pleased to see you undertake this environmental mission to clarify high-priority issues. I've discussed the project with Sharon Kline and Alan Jones, and both of them praised your efforts and recommended I contact you.

I read your article in *The Washington Post* and agree with your stand on the tax issues. I am interested in specializing in taxation and would like an opportunity to discuss these issues with you.

I understand from Ann Parke that your office is presently seeking an Assistant Project Manager. I am interested in applying for the position and request the opportunity to speak with you or one of your associates in the next few weeks.

Now that I have completed my Master's of Science in Accounting, I am exploring the auditing field. I would like to be able to utilize my analytical skills to help corporations improve their operations.

Our mutual friend Mary Worth suggested I contact you during my exploration of e-commerce. This area of marketing excites me and Mary says you are an expert in this field. I will call you next week and promise to take just a few minutes of your time.

Robert Fullen told me you were searching for an IT Manager. He suggested that my qualifications matched your requirements and recommended I explore this opening with you.

While attending the national AARP convention last week, Jeffrey Hudson, whom I have worked with on many regional and national projects, detailed your search plans for the Finance Director position. I am a supporter of AARP's mission and am interested in exploring this opportunity.

You have quite a supporter in Margery Osborne. She persuaded me that the market is ripe for your new restaurant concept. I am intrigued and would like to learn more about your staffing needs.

You were referred to me by Isabel Torres. She gave me a wonderful overview of your expansion into South America and I am keenly interested in working for XYZ in a South American assignment.

Your name keeps surfacing as the most knowledgeable professional in Baltimore on restaurant development. I am exploring a new concept and would be most appreciative if I could speak with you and get some feedback on my immediate plans.

Sample Referral Letters

Here are ten sample referral letters to use as models.

BELINDA WALTON
80 Ortega Court, San Diego, California 92100 (714) XXX-XXXX

August 23, 20XX

United Plastics
Judith Diaz, President
San Buenavista Boulevard
Culver City, CA 90230

Dear Ms. Diaz:

Thomas Fan suggested I contact you concerning the Vice President of Sales and Marketing opportunity. He discussed the position with me and I was struck by the similarity between your requirements and my background.

My extensive experience in sales and marketing management has resulted in expanded markets and increased corporate profits. What I have done for my previous employers, I can do for you.

Sales and Profits
Assumed responsibility for Southwest Region of office equipment corporation. Increased sales from an initial flat $12 million to $22 million level. Generated 25% return on revenue, the highest in the company, contributing an estimated 22% of total company profits.

Human Resources
Reorganized sales operation and expanded staff from 25 to 53. Initiated and conducted training programs; reduced staff turnover 50%. Recognized for "superior leadership skills."

Business Development
Highly successful in developing new business opportunities. Created marketing and advertising programs that targeted and increased sales in commercial and international markets. The enclosed résumé details additional qualifications.

I am interested in taking on a new challenge and excited about the possibility of joining the United Plastics team. I would like to meet with you and discuss how I can help United Plastics reach its sales and marketing goals.

Yours truly,

Belinda Walton

Enclosure

MARK CONNORS
46 Highland Road, San Mateo, California 94400
(415) XXX-XXXX

January 11, 20XX

Travel Unlimited
Sarah Wilson
General Manager
200 Alhambra Street
Carmichael, CA 95600

Dear Ms. Wilson:

Roger Keeler has enthusiastically described your organization and recommended I contact you concerning employment possibilities. I would like to be part of a small, customer-oriented organization that provides superior service.

Highlights of my background and achievements, as outlined in the enclosed résumé, include:

- Four years' experience as a Travel Consultant handling international computer reservations and itineraries.
- Two years' experience generating and servicing corporate accounts.
- Expertise with the Sabre and Cobra computer systems.
- Fluent in Spanish and French and conversant in Italian.

My strongest assets are my interpersonal skills and my love of working with people to make their travel experiences pleasurable.

I'd like to meet with you to learn more about your plans and discuss how I can support your future goals. I'll call to schedule an appointment.

I'll speak with you soon.

Sincerely yours,

Mark Connors

Encl.

ALLAN GILLEN
621 Bayberry Lane
New Rochelle, New York 10804
(914) XXX-XXXX

October 8, 20XX

Klineman Jones
Sarah Miner
800 Sixth Avenue
New York, NY 10004

Dear Sarah:

It's been months since we've been in touch and I wanted to bring you up-to-date on my plans since we last spoke. I have held the Operations Manager position at DFG Incorporated for the last three years. The manufacturing project I launched is near completion and I am currently exploring new opportunities in the metropolitan area.

At this point I am initiating an exploratory search and would like to speak with individuals in different industries that might need my qualifications and skills.

Let me assure you that I am not expecting anyone to provide job leads. Instead, I would like to speak with individuals just like you who have industry knowledge and are willing to share it with me.

I will give you a call within the next week and will only take a few minutes of your time. I wanted to update you first with this letter and give you time to think of any suggestions that may help my search.

Thank you for your time. I'm looking forward to speaking with you.

Sincerely,

Allan Gillen

RANDY FISCHER

321 Dudley Avenue
Kensington, Maryland 20890
(301) XXX-XXXX

May 30, 20XX

Harriet O'Malley
The O'Malley Group
76 Reston Parkway
Reston, VA 20194

Dear Ms. O'Malley:

I heard you speak at the Institute for Internal Auditors convention in Washington, D.C. last week. Your knowledge of Internet applications for auditing was impressive. Of all the programs I attended, yours was by far the best. Your content and presentation were superb. Thanks so much for taking the time to update us on the latest auditing tools.

My background is in auditing within the corporate sector. I've been with my current organization five years and am beginning to explore new options within the auditing field.

You mentioned that you would be willing to recommend opportunities that utilize the new technology. I would like to take you up on that offer. I will give you a call next week and promise to take just a few minutes of your time. If that is not convenient, you can reach me at (301) XXX-XXXX during the day or (301) XXX-XXXX in the evening.

The auditing profession is fortunate to have you as an advocate. I truly appreciate your commitment and willingness to upgrade our skills and knowledge.

I will speak with you soon.

Sincerely,

Randy Fischer

Teresa Logan, CIA
_____

56 Camelia Way, Orlando, Florida 32800 (888) XXX-XXXX

July 5, 20XX

Millie Miller, CPA
American Automobile Association
Parkwood Drive
Orlando, FL 32802

Dear Ms. Miller:

Amelia Henry recommended I contact you concerning the Auditor position you advertised in the July 1, 20XX _Orlando Sentinel._

I have four years' experience as an Auditor for ABC Corporation, where I plan and perform effective operational, compliance, program, and financial audits.

My strong analytical, interpersonal, and communication skills have enabled me to gain expertise in developing audit findings and writing and editing audit reports.

The Auditor position is in line with my career goals, as outlined in the enclosed résumé. I would like to meet with you to discuss how my qualifications can meet your needs. I will call you to schedule a convenient time.

Thank you for your consideration.

Yours truly,

Teresa Logan, CIA

Encl.

JERRY LIVINGSTON
1224 Wilde Lake, Columbia, Maryland 21044
Home (410) XXX-XXXX Work (301) XXX-XXXX

March 15, 20XX

Globalcom
Richard Pippen
Major Accounts Branch Manager
66 River Road
Bethesda, MD 20814

Dear Mr. Pippen:

Heather Black has spoken very highly of you and suggested I contact you concerning sales opportunities within the Major Accounts Branch. I have been impressed with Globalcom's acquisition strategy and would like to utilize my talents in helping your team achieve its goals.

For the past four years I have successfully sold hardware and software solutions to corporate and government accounts. I have a proven record in building client relationships with senior executives. Highlights of my qualifications, as detailed in the enclosed résumé, include:

- Top performance in sales and business development.
- Strong understanding of the telecommunications industry.
- Exceptional communication, interpersonal, and negotiation skills.

It's impossible to convey my enthusiasm and interest on paper. I'm available to meet with you in person to discuss my credentials and your needs. I will call you to schedule a meeting.

Sincerely yours,

Jerry Livingston

Enclosure

MARSHA MONK
9001 North Avenue, Phoenix, Arizona 85100
(602) XXX-XXXX

February 28, 20XX

Desert Foods
Mr. Ross Shivilly
Chief Executive Officer
3 Arrowsmith Drive
Phoenix, AZ 85007

Dear Mr. Shivilly:

Fred Castillo recommended that I contact you concerning the newly created Communications Manager position. A solid background in all aspects of communications makes me confident I would be a productive addition to your management team.

The enclosed résumé highlights my background and achievements:

Six years of experience guiding the development of marketing materials, publications, and speeches for a leader in mortgage financing

Cultivation of an extensive network of national and local media contacts

Proven record in devising marketing and public relations strategies that consistently capture media attention

Expertise in Web site development

Bachelor of Arts in Communications

I'd welcome the opportunity to meet with you in person to share our goals and discuss how I can support your organization.

Yours truly,

Marsha Monk

Enclosure

SAMANTHA ANNE SMITHERS
76 Golden Lane, Columbus, Ohio 43210
(614) XXX-XXXX

January 31, 20XX

The Greasy Spoon
Louise Lettice
Owner/President
6113 Central Avenue
Columbus, OH 43215

Dear Ms. Lettice:

Karen Jones praises your restaurant and suggested I contact you concerning the general manager opportunity.

My five years of experience in all facets of restaurant operations qualifies me for the position. As the manager of the Silver Dollar restaurant, I hired, trained, and supervised staffs of 28 to 30. Selected accomplishments include:

- Reduced staff turnover and stabilized the workforce by promoting from within, delegating responsibility, and recognizing performance.
- Increased sales by successfully coordinating local-store marketing and new product development.
- Established procedures for a new take-out and delivery system.

If you're seeking an innovative, organized manager with exceptional people skills, please consider me a candidate. Details of my credentials are highlighted in the enclosed résumé.

I am available to meet with you to discuss how I can contribute to the success of your operation. I will give you a call to set up an appointment.

Yours truly,

Samantha Anne Smithers

Encl.

JACOB SCHIFF
856 Park Avenue
Philadelphia, Pennsylvania 19128
(215) XXX-XXXX

December 1, 20XX

Catherine Houston
12 Maple Avenue
Philadelphia, PA 19100

Dear Catherine:

Our mutual friend, Abigail Foote, suggested I contact you concerning executive recruiters. She shared your success with your recent job transition and mentioned how satisfied you were with the process.

I am currently the Controller of a large utility company that is planning a major merger. While I enjoy my responsibilities, the work environment has changed and I have begun exploring new opportunities. I haven't looked for a new position in quite some time and would like to use an executive recruiter.

It would be very helpful to speak with you and discuss your search. I will give you a call in a few days to find a time that would be convenient. I look forward to speaking with you.

Thank you for your time.

Very truly yours,

Jacob Schiff

CARL W. KIRK

4119 Cathedral Avenue, Columbus, Ohio 43200 (614) XXX-XXXX

March 4, 20XX

Mary-Ellen Morris
Trainer
Horace and Jones, Ltd.
87 East Second Street
Columbus, OH 43211

Dear Mary-Ellen:

I learned so much at your Leadership Strategies workshop in February. You are an excellent trainer and your presentations made the content come alive.

Since my return to work I have applied a number of the techniques you recommended and the results are impressive. You made a true distinction between managers and leaders and I can already see the positive improvements in my performance.

You mentioned during the workshop that you are familiar with the management philosophy and organizational structure of many companies based in Columbus. I am currently in the process of exploring new opportunities and would like to hear your thoughts on some of the companies I have selected.

I promise to take no more than 15 minutes of your time. I am not asking for help to find a job, just some insight into the management philosophy of a few companies.

I will give you a call later this week to find a convenient time for us to speak.

Thank you so much for your insight and inspiration. You've already made a big difference in my life. I look forward to speaking with you soon.

Sincerely yours,

Carl W. Kirk

Writing Gracious Thank-You Letters

10

Good manners dictate that we thank others for their help and support. In this fast-paced, quick-touch world, a sincere and formal thank you delivers a powerful impression. Thank-you letters provide you the opportunity to follow up on a phone or personal interview with a subtle reminder of your interest and qualifications.

You'll place yourself ahead of the competition if you compose thoughtful and effective letters. While most job seekers are aware of how important thank-you letters are, many neglect to use them.

It's rare that an individual pulls off a successful job search or transition on his or her own; usually a large supporting cast paves the way with ideas, recommendations, introductions, and referrals. You'll use thank-you letters to express appreciation to all who helped you.

 in Thank-You Letters

- STEP 1: Open your letter with an introductory sentence that expresses appreciation to the recipient.
- STEP 2: Comment on what you learned or the benefit you received from either the interviewer or the recipient.
- STEP 3: In the central part of your interview-directed letter, mention how your credentials match the job opportunity.

- STEP 4: In other thank-you letters, explain how the support has helped your job search and career plans.
- STEP 5: Include any additional information that helps position you for jobs of interest.
- STEP 6: Craft a strong close detailing your appreciation and interest.

in Thank-You Letters

- Avoid sounding ambivalent, uncertain, or indicating indecision about whether this position or organization is really a match for you.
- Do not include any statement that suggests a lack of confidence on your part or any concerns about your ability to perform the job.
- Spelling, grammar, or punctuation errors will knock you out of the running—no matter how welcome your letter.

Tips on Writing Thank-You Letters

1. Thank-you letters can be either typewritten or handwritten; this is the only type of job search letter that *can* be handwritten.
2. Send your letters within 24 hours. If you can't do this, send a thank-you message by electronic mail (see Chapter 6). Follow up the message with either a typed or handwritten letter.
3. While it is often acceptable to send a thank-you letter by electronic mail for positions in the technical industries, use typed or handwritten letters for other positions and industries.
4. Show a match between the requirements identified during the interview and your experience and accomplishments.
5. Express a strong interest in the organization and position.
6. Add any related accomplishments and experience not discussed in the interview.
7. When sending typewritten letters, follow the business letter writing instructions in Chapter 4.

Tip: It's professional to use the same paper for all your job search correspondence, but it's not essential. If using a different paper, stay with $8\frac{1}{2} \times 11$-inch, 24-pound paper in conservative colors.

8. Some people prefer to write their thank-you notes by hand and note cards are appropriate for this purpose. Select simple and classic papers, either plain or personalized.

Tip: Minimize mistakes by writing out your text on plain paper and copying it on the cards.

Special Situations

~ You had interviews with four different managers from the company. Send a letter to the manager who coordinated the interview process and ask that your appreciation be shared with the other three interviewers. Or, write a different letter to each interviewer.

~ You're not sure if you want the job. A simple thank-you is always appreciated and in no way commits you to either the organization or opportunity. It always pays to leave a good impression.

~ You forgot to send a thank-you letter and a week has passed. If you are interested in the position, write your thank-you letter and get it in the mail immediately.

Tip: Don't apologize; it will only draw attention that the letter is late.

~ The interviewer ended the interview by stating "We are looking for someone with more ** experience." If you feel you are qualified for the job and want to pursue it, use the thank-you letter as an opportunity to detail how your qualifications match the stated job requirements. Mention that you would be willing to meet with them again to further discuss how you can manage the position's responsibilities.

Words to Use in Thank-You Letters

again	enjoyed	interview	pleasure	support
appreciate	exactly	liked	possibility	taking
assistance	excited	match	quick	thank
challenging	for	meeting	rewarding	time
contact	impressed	note	seeking	you
conversation	interest			

Phrases to Use in Thank-You Letters

enjoyed meeting you

express my appreciation

hear from you

it was a pleasure

let's get together

look forward

making a decision

provide additional information

thank you again

wonderful to see you

your support made the difference

Sentences to Use in Thank-You Letters

I am very interested in becoming part of your management team.

I appreciate your making time for me in your busy schedule.

I couldn't have done it without your help.

I look forward to speaking with you again soon.

I thoroughly enjoyed the opportunity to meet your staff and tour the Customer Service Center.

Please let me know how I can help you in the future.

Should you need additional information, please feel free to contact me at (888) XXX-XXXX.

Thank you for taking time from your busy schedule.

Thanks so much for all your help.

Your resource was exactly the help I needed.

Paragraphs to Use in Thank-You Letters

How fortunate I am to have a colleague like you. Your help made all the difference in bringing my search to a successful close. I knew I could count on you and I hope you'll let me reciprocate in the future.

I want to thank you for taking time out of your busy schedule to interview me last Monday. The production strategies you shared are truly innovative and it's easy to catch your enthusiasm. I am eager to join your team and contribute to this new project.

It was a pleasure to meet with you and Stephanie Allen on Wednesday. I thoroughly enjoyed learning about your expansion plans and would like to be a part of your team. This position is exactly what I have been seeking. I hope you are as enthusiastic about my qualifications as I am about your organization.

Mr. Henry was a valuable resource. He shared a number of potential contacts with me and provided three personal referrals. Thanks so much for your help in reaching him. I feel confident this job search will be fruitful. I will update you on my progress.

Sample Thank-You Letters

Here are five examples of thank-you letters.

Kathleen Robbins
643 Shellview Way
Plantation, Florida 33320
(954) XXX-XXXX

April 4, 20XX

Office of the District Attorney
Carlos Gonzales
Chief Trial Deputy
2 Market Square
Miami, FL 33100

Dear Mr. Gonzales:

Thank you for meeting with me on Monday. Speaking with you and learning more about the work you do reaffirmed my interest in a career with the Miami District Attorney's Office.

I was especially intrigued with the work you are doing, not only to prevent crime, but to promote victims' rights. My five years of prosecution experience will enable me to quickly participate in your pending cases.

I am very excited about your goals and would like to be a part of your team, using my skills to represent the City of Miami.

Thanks again for your consideration.

Very truly yours,

Kathleen Robbins

7221 Hillview Court, Phoenix, Arizona 85100
(602) XXX-XXXX

May 13, 20XX

Alpha Corporation
Samuel Sheldon
98 Sandlewood Lane
Phoenix, AZ 85102

Dear Mr. Sheldon:

Thank you for taking the time to meet with me on Tuesday and discussing the Trainer/Marketing Assistant position.

This job is an exact match for my skills and experience and I'm excited about the opportunity. My eight years of diverse training experience will enable me to:

Develop and Coordinate Training Programs: More than five years of experience designing, coordinating, and delivering training programs for diverse corporate and public sector clients.

Standardize Training Programs: More than five years of experience standardizing, coordinating, and delivering Zenger Miller training programs for a large corporation.

Act as a Resource for Staff Training Issues: More than 12 years of training experience including five years of train-the-trainer experience. A dedicated team player with a commitment to support organizational goals.

Should you have additional questions for me, please call me at (602) XXX-XXXX. I am very interested in this position and look forward to speaking with you again.

Sincerely,

Dane White

TYRONE ADAMS
3445 Station Way
Lincoln, Nebraska 68500
(402) XXX-XXXX

June 14, 20XX

Technical Solutions
Michelle Apple
Program Manager
61 Fourth Street
Lincoln, NE 68400

Dear Michelle:

It was a pleasure meeting you on Thursday and learning more about your company.

I came away from our meeting knowing I would be a productive member of your team and an asset to Technical Solutions. My skills and background match closely with your company's growing need for experienced application programmers and I believe I possess the talent, commitment, and continuity you are seeking in prospective team members.

I'm very excited about the position as it will utilize my technical skills while enhancing my networking experience. Please keep me in mind as you make your staffing decision.

Thank you again for your time on Thursday.

Sincerely yours,

Tyrone Adams

CAITLIN MARSHALL
65 Main Street, Apartment 15, Rockville, Maryland 20850
(301) XXX-XXXX   Home (301) XXX-XXXX Work

March 1, 20XX

Montgomery County
Anthony Wagner, Director
7 Maxwell Street
Suite 111
Rockville, MD 20800

Dear Mr. Wagner:

I enjoyed meeting with you and Diedre Small last Tuesday and discussing the Program Manager opportunity. I have been a lifelong advocate for women's rights and would enjoy the challenge of making a difference in the community while utilizing my skills and expertise.

My extensive social service background provides me with the tools to create, execute, and manage programs to benefit women in Montgomery County. Highlights of my qualifications include:

- Team player with a proven record of working effectively with diverse and multicultural populations.
- Flexible and adaptable performer with exceptional strategic planning and project management skills.
- Extensive experience in conceptualizing and delivering programs to help women at risk in the areas of domestic violence, sexual assault prevention, self-esteem, and life skills.

I am very interested in working in an area that ties in with my beliefs and would enjoy helping Montgomery County achieve its goals.

Sincerely yours,

Caitlin Marshall

Felix Carthage
909 Poplar Lane
Topeka, Kansas 66600
(913) XXX-XXXX

November 20, 20XX

Lester Barillo
Hawthorne Limited
42 Mellow Road
Topeka, KS 66611

Dear Lester:

Thanks so much for sharing the job lead for a Systems Engineer at Meredith Industries.

I met with John Sullivan on Wednesday and the interview went well. My qualifications are a match for the job and they seem interested in me. They plan to make a decision by the 30th and I will let you know what transpires.

I enjoyed catching up with you at the TechNow Conference last week. Let's plan to meet for lunch after the holiday—my treat.

Your support is really appreciated, Lester. Thanks again for all your help.

Sincerely,

Felix Carthage

Using Follow-Up Letters to Get Results

11

Many job seekers delay success by taking a passive approach. It is essential that you follow up on all leads and interviews to bring your job search to a positive end.

The follow-up letter reminds the recipient of your qualifications and goals and reinforces your interest in the position or organization. It's also an excellent vehicle to report back to your contacts on what you've accomplished, based on their suggestions. Once your search is complete, follow-up letters provide a link to your network and any others who helped during the search.

 in Follow-Up Letters

- STEP 1: State the purpose of your letter in the first paragraph. You might remind the employer that you are still in the job market, demonstrate interest in a specific position, or ask to be considered should an appropriate opening occur. When writing to your contacts, you'll disclose the status or outcome of your search.

- STEP 2: Share information about yourself in the middle paragraphs, either positions offered, accepted, or being considered. When still searching, mention the qualities and accomplishments that should interest an employer.

- STEP 3: End your letter by requesting they review, evaluate, or consider your qualifications.

Tip: Clearly ask for what you'd like—a phone call, meeting, or consideration for a current or future opening.

- STEP 4: Express appreciation for their help and support in the job search.

 ## in Follow-Up Letters

- You're frustrated that you have yet to find a job.
- You don't understand why you weren't selected for an opening.
- You are disappointed the organization has yet to make a decision.
- Resources provided to you were not helpful.
- Complaints about the search length or outcomes.

Tips on Writing Follow-Up Letters

1. Keep your letter upbeat.
2. Highlight credentials or accomplishments not stated in other correspondence.
3. Look for an article of interest based on previous conversations and use that as an opening for your correspondence.

Special Situations

You've interviewed for a job and when you followed up, you were told there was a hiring freeze. Communicate your interest to the hiring manager and follow up periodically with phone calls or brief letters. If you are a top candidate, the manager will be pleased to know of your continued interest.

You were told the organization would make a decision in two weeks and that was three weeks ago. Follow up with a phone call and ask if a decision has been made. If it hasn't, follow up with a brief letter stating your interest and your qualifications for the position.

∾ *You met someone at a conference who works for an organization that you're interested in.* Write a follow-up letter expressing your pleasure in meeting him or her, your interest in the organization, and a desire to keep in touch to learn of organizational opportunities.

∾ *You interviewed with an organization over two months ago and you are still looking.* You've probably updated your résumé based on suggestions from interviewers and colleagues. Write a letter that demonstrates your continued interest in employment and provide a revised copy of your résumé.

Words to Use in Follow-Up Letters

accepted	confirm	interest	secured	status
appreciate	copy	meet	seeking	still
assumed	enclosing	openings	select	talk
aware	enjoyed	opportunities	share	update
commence	inform	remind		

Phrases to Use in Follow-Up Letters

appreciate your encouragement

enjoyed meeting you

I would like your feedback

interested in working for ABC

landed a new job

located a wonderful opportunity

per our discussion

should you be aware of openings

sincerely interested in

still actively looking

still interested in the position

thanks so much

update you on my progress

your support is appreciated

Sentences to Use in Follow-Up Letters

I am still interested in the position.

I feel there is a match between my expertise and your requirements.

It was a pleasure having lunch with you at the XYZ conference.

I've recently updated my résumé to reflect my current assignment and I've enclosed a copy for your review.

My experience is compatible with the requirements you shared.

Now that I've met your staff, I know we'd make a good team.

Please let me know when you've made a decision.

The new position is exactly what I wanted.

Paragraphs to Use in Follow-Up Letters

I was so energized after our meeting that I took the time to outline some suggestions for the office relocation. The three moves I orchestrated for XYZ Inc. gave me insight into the most efficient methods that minimize operational disruptions. I'd like to meet with you again to share my ideas.

Thank you for taking the time to share industry trends with me last week. I've enclosed a copy of an article from the *Denver Bulletin* that details the Internet service you discussed. Technology is a special interest of mine and I would like to be considered for the promotional position when it becomes available.

The last time we spoke, you mentioned it might be another four weeks until a decision was made for the program coordinator opening. Based on the programming needs you identified during our interview, I have drafted a proposal for the upcoming annual conference. I would be happy to meet with you again and share my ideas for conference programming.

While I understand ABC Company is experiencing a two-month hiring freeze, I would like to be considered for the stock analyst position when you commence hiring. As we previously discussed, my experience and skills are the right mix for the described requirements.

Sample Follow-Up Letters

Here are four examples of follow-up letters.

JEAN COLLIER
2114 Lovell Lane
Pittsburgh, Pennsylvania 15211
(412) XXX-XXXX

May 11, 20XX

Milton Industries
Jane Hood
Director of Administration
45 Old Wood Road
Pittsburgh, PA 15200

Dear Jane:

You were a wonderful help during my recent search and I wanted to share my good news with you.

I accepted a Billing Manager position with New Technologies, effective June 2. It is exactly the opportunity I wanted; an excellent blend of management and technology plus the challenge of learning new products and systems. I am thrilled and ready to begin this new phase of my career.

I can't thank you enough, Jane, for your ideas and support throughout the search. I promise to keep in touch and eagerly anticipate reciprocating your generosity in the near future.

Sincerely,

Jean Collier

LOUIS WILDER
800 Mountain Road
Bangor, Maine 04400
(207) XXX-XXXX

July 10, 20XX

Pitney Jones, Inc.
Mr. Jonathan Irons
6432 Church Street
Bangor, ME 04411

Dear Mr. Irons:

It's been several months since we've been in touch. I am still searching for an account executive opportunity, pursuing all leads to market and sell technology products.

I've revised my résumé to reflect a stronger technology background, highlighting the completion of three recent courses. The classroom and hands-on applications training increased my knowledge of product capabilities. I will be able to use this information to more convincingly sell clients on technological advantages.

A copy of my new résumé is enclosed. I have continued interest in Pitney Jones, Inc. and will call you next week to discuss your staffing plans.

Thank you for your continued interest and support. I look forward to speaking with you.

Sincerely yours,

Louis Wilder

Enclosure

HEATHER COULTER

8990 Stepping Stone Court
Sacramento, California 95800
(916) XXX-XXXX

September 15, 20XX

Kings Limited
Stefanie Adams
361 Center Avenue
Sacramento, CA 95811

Dear Ms. Adams:

I wanted to let you know that I am still interested in the publicity and marketing relations position at Kings Limited. I am aware that the hiring freeze will be in effect for another month, but I would like to be considered for the position once you have approval to hire.

In the past three months I have explored many opportunities but I always come back to Kings Limited. Your position most closely matches my qualifications and career goals. I'm energized at the prospect of building a public relations and marketing function and I am committed to bringing media exposure to Kings Limited.

I am willing to wait for your hiring decision and will keep in touch.

Thank you for your continued interest.

Sincerely,

Heather Coulter

Merrill T. Lansing
7993 Golden Square
San Francisco, California 94104
(415) XXX-XXXX

April 15, 20XX

XYZ International
Elizabeth Hilton
Operations Manager
759 Third Avenue
San Francisco, CA 94100

Dear Ms. Hilton:

I enjoyed meeting with you in early March and discussing the planned expansions in your operations function. At the time we met, you were in the preliminary stage of establishing a new operations position and suggested I follow up with you in a month once the position was approved.

During this period I have given a great deal of thought to your plans and how they relate to my qualifications. The position would draw on my eight years of manufacturing and sales experience plus my skills and training. The more I think about it, the more excited I get. The prospect of linking manufacturing, sales, and administration in a leading-edge environment is a wonderful challenge and I would like to be the one to do it.

I have revised my résumé since we met and have enclosed an updated copy. I will give you a call this week to discuss your staffing plans. Thanks so much for all your help and encouragement.

I'll speak with you soon.

Yours truly,

Merrill T. Lansing

Enclosure

Accepting or Declining the Job Offer

12

After months of interviewing and job search angst, an offer finally arrives. Whether it's the offer of your dreams or one of little interest, it needs both a decision and a written response.

It is very important that you document any offer you negotiate and accept. If you don't have all the details in writing—starting salary, start date, first evaluation, salary range, and any negotiated exceptions such as vacation time or benefit package—it is possible that when you arrive for your first day, you may find yourself with salary and benefits less than agreed upon.

When an offer is extended that you do not want to accept, or if you have several offers to consider, let an organization know as quickly as possible that you will not be accepting its offer so it can fill the position.

 How to Say It in Acceptance or Decline Letters

- STEP 1: State in your first paragraph that you are confirming acceptance of the offer and include the position title and the effective date.
- STEP 2: When declining an offer, begin your first paragraph by stating your regret in not accepting the position.
- STEP 3: Express your enthusiasm about accepting the position or your appreciation in the organization's interest when declining the position.

- STEP 4: Reiterate all salary and evaluation details or refer to the offer letter prepared by the organization.
- STEP 5: Close your letter on a positive note, either expressing excitement for the offer or, when declining, your regret in not accepting the offer and wishing the organization well.

in Acceptance or Decline Letters

- The offer wasn't very good.
- The job wasn't what you wanted.
- You've found a better job.
- You plan to work for a competitor.
- You'll accept an offer before finalizing salary and benefit details.

Tips on Writing Acceptance or Decline Letters

1. Write your letter as soon as you've made a decision about the offer.
2. Be positive and leave the door open.

Tip: It pays to be cordial. There are instances when applicants refused job offers only to pursue openings with the organization in the future.

3. Show appreciation for the organization's interest.
4. Document every detail to ensure you are clear on all points prior to employment.
5. Provide any additional information the organization has requested.

Special Situations

∿ *The organization has not given you all the particulars.* It is in your best interests to follow up immediately with either human resources or the hiring manager to identify starting salary, start date, first evaluation, salary range, and benefit package.

∼ *The organization has not provided a written offer.* Continue to pursue a written confirmation of the offer. It is best if the confirmation comes from the organization on its letterhead. If you are unable to get a written confirmation, prepare one yourself following the sample on page 210.

∼ *You are pressured to make a decision before you are willing to commit.* Compose a stall letter (see example on page 212). While the organization has no obligation to extend its deadline, you may request more time to make your decision. Ask for more time, indicating the additional time needed or the date you'll make a decision. You need not state why you need the additional time.

Words to Use in Acceptance or Decline Letters

accept	excited	interview	regret
confirm	forward	offer	resign
decline	happy	pleasure	tended
disappointed	hear	position	unable

Phrases to Use in Acceptance or Decline Letters

accept your offer	I will be unable to accept
after much consideration	pleased to accept
appreciate your offer	regret that I am unable
available immediately	sincerely appreciate your efforts
I am quite pleased	thank you for your letter
I can begin work on	thank you for your offer

Sentences to Use in Acceptance or Decline Letters

I am confident I will make a favorable impression for the January 2, 20XX performance review you mentioned.

I am grateful for the time and effort spent on my behalf.

I am pleased to accept your offer for the Chief Accountant position.

I appreciate your interest but must decline your offer for the Marketing Director position.

I regret I must decline your offer.

I look forward to getting started.

I understand that I will be reporting to Mary Miller on March 1, 20XX.

My employer requires two weeks' notice which makes me available on May 15.

Perhaps our paths will cross again in the future.

Please confirm the offer in writing.

Thank you for the opportunity you presented.

Thank you once again for your offer.

Thanks for all the time you spent with me.

Unfortunately I have accepted another position.

Paragraphs to Use in Acceptance or Decline Letters

I am pleased to accept your offer for the Administrator position. I will give my employer two weeks' notice and will be available as of January 20.

Thanks so much for your confidence. I am excited about the Regional Manager position and look forward to joining the management team.

While your offer for the securities position matched most of the elements I am seeking, in the final analysis I decided to accept an offer from another organization. I wanted to share with you my decision as quickly as possible so you can offer this opportunity to another qualified candidate.

Your offer for the Executive Assistant position is flattering. However, I must decline the opportunity as I have decided to relocate to New York.

Sample Acceptance, Decline, or Stall Letters

Take a look at the following four sample letters.

Melissa Shapiro

89 Main Street
Culver City, California 90230
(310) XXX-XXXX

November 1, 20XX

Techno Center
Ms. Klein
Director, Human Resources
75 Elm Street
Culver City, CA 90234

Dear Ms. Klein:

I am very pleased to accept your employment offer as an instructional designer within the Leadership Initiative Center at Techno Center. I am eager to join the management team and work at such a progressive and reputable center.

I appreciate your confidence in my skills and want to assure you that I will do my best to contribute to your business objectives.

I will submit my formal resignation to my current employer today and look forward to beginning work on December 10, 20XX.

As you requested, I have signed and enclosed the offer letter.

Again, thank you for providing me with this opportunity. I look forward to fulfilling your expectations.

Sincerely yours,

Melissa Shapiro

4767 West Allen Lane, Charleston, West Virginia 25304 (304) XXX-XXXX

June 2, 20XX

XYY Company
Eldon Jacobs
Director of Personnel
2 Main Street
Charleston, WV 25300

Dear Mr. Jacobs:

This will confirm your offer to me for the position of Billing Manager, effective July 1, 20XX. I was happy to hear from you and want to accept your offer.

The salary for the position is $4,000 per month. My first review date will be July 1, 20XX. The salary range for this position is:

Minimum	Midpoint	Maximum
$3,800	$4,500	$5,200

I am excited about the challenge this position presents and look forward to working with you.

Very truly yours,

Larry Peters

Harold Smith
One Maxwell Road
Baltimore, Maryland 21233
(410) XXX-XXXX

March 2, 20XX

National Telecommunications
Mr. David Holt
Regional Sales Manager
87 Commons Drive
Baltimore, MD 21200

Dear Mr. Holt:

I enjoyed meeting with you and your staff and appreciate your recent offer for a Systems Coordinator position.

After much consideration, I have decided to accept a systems support opportunity in a different industry. This position more closely matches my present career objectives.

Thank you for all your efforts on my behalf. I wish you and your group continued success.

Sincerely yours,

Harold Smith

Zachary Oliver
84 Statute Lane, #201
Wheaton, Maryland 20900
(301) XXX-XXXX

October 2, 20XX

XYZ Technologies, Inc.
Mary Smith
Director, Human Resources
9 Main Street
Wheaton, MD 20905

Dear Ms. Smith:

Thank you for your offer for the position of Executive Assistant to the President. I appreciate the time and effort you've spent on my behalf and I'm excited about the opportunity.

You've requested I make a decision on this offer by October 8. This is such an important decision and I would like more time to evaluate my options. I do not believe that I can make the decision by October 8. However, I will have a response to your offer by November 1 and would appreciate an extension until that date.

Once again, thank you for this opportunity. I look forward to your reply.

Sincerely yours,

Zachary Oliver

Preparing Letters of Resignation

13

When it is time to move on to another organization or make a transition into a new life experience, it is important to leave your current position on a positive note. No matter what your work experience, leave gracefully. Never burn bridges; you may need to interact with this organization or some of the employees in future business endeavors or you may need them as a future reference.

 in Resignation Letters

- STEP 1: Craft an introductory paragraph that states your intent to resign and its effective date.
- STEP 2: State your reasons for leaving in a second paragraph, such as relocation, return to school, retirement, or new opportunity.

Tip: You are under no obligation to provide details or elaborate on your plans.

- STEP 3: End your letter on an upbeat note and, if appropriate, indicate your appreciation for support and a statement about your experience with the organization.

Tip: Always use a positive and professional tone when tendering your resignation.

in Resignation Letters

- Refrain from saying, "I quit."
- Avoid using an unpleasant or disagreeable tone.
- Resist divulging negative comments about the organization or specific employees.
- Put aside adverse thoughts about your work experience.
- It is not appropriate to detail your feelings; keep the letter impersonal.

Tips on Writing Resignation Letters

1. Just stick to the facts.
2. Keep your emotions at bay.
3. There is no need to apologize.
4. Despite how you may be feeling, bear in mind that a resignation letter is not an opportunity to settle old scores; it is simply a document to confirm your intent to leave the organization.
5. There is no requirement that you must identify your new employer or explain your future plans.

Special Situations

~ *You're being pressured to resign.* Keep your letter short but confirm the date of your resignation and any specifics such as the period for severance pay, benefits, or vacation.

~ *You've had a bad experience.* It's important to remain professional and leave on a positive note. You may need to work with former supervisors, colleagues, or subordinates through professional associations, industry events, or at another organization.

~ *You are thrilled to be leaving.* Rein in your jubilation and state your intent, departure date, and a short statement of appreciation.

~ *You are retiring.* Work with your human resources or the appropriate department to ensure your retirement plan meets organizational requirements.

Words to Use in Resignation Letters

accepted	express	replacement
appreciate	formal	resign
confirm	inform	resignation
courtesy	notice	sincere
effective	regret	

Phrases to Use in Resignation Letters

appreciate your support	keep in touch
best wishes for the future	my last day of work
effective December 1, 20XX	thank you again
express my appreciation	thank you for your help
I have accepted	this will confirm
if I can help	

Sentences to Use in Resignation Letters

As we discussed this morning, I have accepted a position at Thomlins Corporation, effective May 7, 20XX.

I hope the two weeks' notice is sufficient.

I will be leaving F&T Incorporated, effective June 5, 20XX.

It's been a pleasure working for you and I plan to keep in touch.

It is with regret that I resign my position with JRT Incorporated, effective July 10, 20XX.

Thank you for your help and guidance during my employment.

This letter is notification of my resignation from AXD, effective November 1, 20XX.

You have been a tremendous support during my years as Branch Administrator.

Paragraphs to Use in Resignation Letters

I appreciate all your efforts on my behalf in soliciting funds for the new accounting program. I am sorry your attempts were unsuccessful as I would have enjoyed working with you on this project.

I understand how difficult this merger has been for all parties and do appreciate the consideration and interest in my appointment as Interim Sales Manager. After much thought I have accepted an offer with another organization and will resign effective January 8, 20XX.

You have been a wonderful manager and I have learned a great deal under your supervision. Unfortunately, the latest acquisition has drastically changed my responsibilities and, regrettably, I have decided to take a position with another firm.

We have previously discussed my desire for additional responsibility, and your insights and suggestions have been valuable. I regret that I had to go outside the organization to find a suitable match.

Sample Resignation Letters

Here are four examples of resignation letters.

8221 Loden Lane, #555
Baltimore, Maryland 21200
(410) XXX-XXXX

December 5, 20XX

Sallingers Inc.
Henry Gibbs
Director of Human Resources
8 Charles Road
Baltimore, MD 21244

Dear Mr. Gibbs:

Please accept this letter as my formal notice of resignation, effective Thursday, December 19, 20XX.

I have secured a new position that offers me the growth and additional responsibility I have been seeking.

I've enjoyed my tenure with Sallingers and appreciate your efforts on my behalf.

Sincerely yours,

Richard West

Lorraine Evers
768 Center Street
Cedar Falls, Iowa 50614
(319) XXX-XXXX

January 2, 20XX

Flora Hill
Century Printing
909 Rocky Road
Cedar Falls, IA 50610

Dear Ms. Hill:

I recently accepted a job offer that provides a wider scope of management duties and long-term career opportunity and will resign my position at Century Printing on January 20, 20XX.

Thank you for all your help and guidance during my career with Century Printing. I have enjoyed working here for the past three years.

Please let me know if I can be of help during the transition or assist in training my replacement.

I appreciate your support and confidence in me. Best wishes for the future.

Sincerely,

Lorraine Evers

MICHAEL W. CRENSHAW
1011 Woodland Court
Armonk, New York 10504
(914) XXX-XXXX

July 14, 20XX

LLN Corporation
Richard Perry
Director of Human Resources
98 Industrial Drive
Armonk, NY 10500

Dear Mr. Perry:

This will confirm my resignation as Chief Financial Officer effective July 15, 20XX.

As we discussed, I will receive severance pay for 16 weeks and my health benefits will continue until December 31, 20XX. My unused vacation and sick pay will be disbursed in a lump sum payment.

I appreciate your support in negotiating these terms.

Sincerely yours,

Michael W. Crenshaw

Bart Longfellow
780 Stately Way
Atlanta, Georgia 30300
(404) XXX-XXXX

August 23, 20XX

Milner Industries
Karl Cohen
Director of Operations
87 High Street
Atlanta, GA 30316

Dear Karl:

This letter confirms our meeting yesterday when I announced my intent to resign my position effective September 15, 20XX.

I have truly enjoyed my seven years with Milner Industries and will miss the many friendships developed over the years. My decision is personal, based on my long commute and the recent opportunity to start my own business.

I am grateful for the opportunities you've provided me and your confidence in my abilities. I'm looking forward to continuing our relationship through collaborative projects in the near future.

Thanks so much for your support. Please let me know if I can help in any way during the transition.

Yours truly,

Bart Longfellow

PART THREE

Making the Best Impression—
Interviews

Preparing for the Interview

Self-Test Your Savvy in Delivering a Positive Impression at an Interview: How Good Are You at Marketing Yourself?

The following self-test is a tool to help you assess whether you are ready to participate in the interview process. The objective is not to get the highest score possible, but to pinpoint areas that you can strengthen to persuade employers of your hireability.

1. I should dress for the job I am interviewing for.   T/F __
2. It's important to research an organization prior to an interview.   T/F __
3. I've interviewed for lots of jobs so I don't think I need to review questions again.   T/F __
4. An interviewer who states, "I just interviewed four other people; what makes you think you're the best?" is really not interested in me.   T/F __
5. I should let my employer know I am looking for a job.   T/F __
6. The main purpose of an interview is for the employer to determine if I am the right candidate for the job.   T/F __
7. It's important for me to relax so I can be my best.   T/F __
8. The most common type of interview is the one-on-one.   T/F __
9. I should bring a list of at least three references to the interview.   T/F __

10. The Internet is a great source for interview directions
  to make sure I don't get lost.   T/F __

11. I'm not afraid of open-ended questions because I can
  answer the question any way I like.   T/F __

12. It's important to make eye contact.   T/F __

13. The job interview is the most crucial step in the job
  search process.   T/F __

14. I should send letters of recommendations prior to my
  interview.   T/F __

15. Interviewers will judge me by my appearance. T/F __

16. When an interviewer begins the interview by asking
  "Can you tell me about yourself," it should prepare
  me for an indirect interview scenario.   T/F __

17. Questions that deal with what, where, when, how, and
  why are direct questions.   T/F __

18. If I send conflicting verbal and nonverbal messages,
  the interviewer is most likely to believe the verbal message. T/F __

19. You never get a second chance to make a first impression. T/F __

20. I should never leave an interview without letting the
  interviewer know that I am really interested in the job. T/F __

21. A good interviewer wants the applicant to do most
  of the talking.   T/F __

22. The best way to answer a question about salary is
  with a question about the salary.   T/F __

23. I should plan to arrive at the interview about
  20 to 30 minutes early.   T/F __

24. I should get permission from my references before
  using them.   T/F __

25. I should practice answering key questions prior
  to the interview.   T/F __

26. The direct interview is a conversation of questions
  and answers.   T/F __

27. Hiring managers prefer to hire people they like. T/F __

28. Interviewers are impressed with applicants who have
  taken the time to prepare for the interview.   T/F __

29. The Internet is a good place to research organizations. T/F __
30. My posture and appearance all send a message before
    I say a word. T/F __
31. An interviewer can ask me any question he or she
    would like. T/F __
32. Open-ended questions can be answered with a "yes"
    or "no." T/F __
33. It's important to appear relaxed during the interview
    and smile when it is appropriate. T/F __
34. Open-ended questions will reveal how I organize my
    thoughts. T/F __
35. If I find myself being interviewed with a group, the
    organization is probably trying to save time. T/F __

Total: _____

Score 1 point for each "True" response and 0 for each "False" response,
EXCEPT for questions 3, 4, 5, 10, 14, 18, 23, 31, 32, 35. *For these questions
only*, **subtract** 1 point for each "True" response. Record your total. A score
below +23 indicates that you would benefit from practicing the interview
techniques discussed in this chapter. (*Note:* It is possible to have a negative
score.)

Interview Fundamentals

The job interview is an opportunity for a potential employer to review your skills, abilities, and accomplishments, and determine if your qualifications match the requirements of the job opening. It's also an opportunity for you, the candidate, to offer your qualifications as well as ask the potential employer questions about the job and organization to help you decide if you are interested in working in this capacity for this organization.

It sounds simple enough, and yet most people dread and sweat through the interview process. A job interview is a time for you to be at your best, so that you can express your strengths and effectively sell yourself. You need to review in an interesting way your past, present, and future; describe what you can bring to the organization, how your qualifications match the requirements, and state why you are the best candidate for the job.

Types of Interviews

Interviews come in all shapes and sizes and you should prepare yourself to deal with a variety of interview types and situations.

ONE-ON-ONE INTERVIEW

1. The most common type of interview; one interviewer interviewing one job candidate.
2. The interviewer will take either a direct or nondirect approach.

DIRECT INTERVIEW

1. Dialogue of questions and answers: The interviewer asks specific questions about your work experience, career goals, education, training, skills, as well as community, personal, and leisure activities, and you provide the responses.
2. Sample questions include:
   How do you hire?
   How do you identify system requirements?

What do you see as potentials in this industry?

What career goals have you set for yourself?

What experience have you had with financial institutions?

NONDIRECT INTERVIEW

1. Less structured interview with the control of both the questions and answers given to the interviewee.
2. Interviewer may begin with "Tell me about yourself," and encourage interviewee with comments such as, "That sounds interesting," or "Can you tell me more about that?"
3. Little direction is provided in this interview situation and you should be prepared to take the ball and run with it.
4. Use the time to describe your qualifications in experience, training, and skills, and demonstrate how you can contribute to both the position and the organization.

STRESS OR DEFENSIVE INTERVIEW

1. Places you in a stressful situation while the interviewer assesses your ability to handle pressure.
2. Often a one-on-one interview.
3. Interviewer may put you in stress immediately: "I just interviewed four candidates; what makes you think you're any good?" Or interviewer establishes a comfortable rapport, then, after you've answered a question, states, "That's the most inefficient way to handle that kind of thing."
4. Often used as a technique to assess how candidates deal with stress when the work environment is a stressful one, such as law enforcement.

Tip: The best response to this strategy is to assertively, calmly, and logically answer and explain your accomplishments. And, if this is not an assessment for a stressful work environment, give serious thought to whether you want to work for an individual or organization that resorts to this type of interview.

PANEL INTERVIEW

1. Brings together two or more interviewers with different perspectives on what they may be looking for in a job candidate.
2. Used most frequently in the public sector.
3. Often composed of a representative from human resources, the hiring manager, employee in a similar position, and/or members of the department.
4. Questions are preselected (the process is known as the patterned approach) and all job candidates are asked the same questions.
5. Each panel member rates each candidate after the interview. When the interview process is completed, the candidates are stack ranked.
6. The candidate with the highest ranking is offered the job.

GROUP INTERVIEW

1. A group of candidates is interviewed at the same time.
2. Often conducted as a panel interview.
3. Offers the interviewers the opportunity to simultaneously assess the interpersonal, communication, and technical skills of several job candidates.
4. Job candidates may all be asked the same question, to be answered separately; or the entire group may be asked a question requiring a group response.

Tip: Be aware of your group interactions. If a group question is asked, the panel will evaluate how each candidate works in a team environment and which candidates take a leadership initiative.

SITUATIONAL INTERVIEW

1. Can be either a one-on-one or panel interview.
2. Interviewer describes a situation and then asks you how you would handle or resolve it.

3. Questions are structured to get information on your experience, skills, attitudes, and abilities.
4. Interviewer will frequently detail a work-related scenario and ask you how you would handle it; for example, "If you were the manager and your best staff member began arriving late, what would you do?"

TARGETED SELECTION INTERVIEW

1. Structured interview technique that seeks answers through real-life experience.
2. Interviewer does not use hypothetical questions but asks instead how you would handle potential real-life problems; for example, "Tell me about a situation you have faced where you discovered fraudulent practices."

SERIAL INTERVIEW

1. Interviewer provides advance notice that applicant will interview with several individuals such as the human resources representative, hiring manager, and divisional manager.
2. Applicant has a favorable interview with the hiring manager. Hiring manager is interested and requests applicant remain for additional interviews with the selection staff who will ultimately collaborate on the hiring decision.
3. While applicant may have been advised the interview will take two hours, it is in the job seeker's best interest to spend as much time as necessary and speak with as many organizational representatives as needed to make a favorable hiring decision.

Tip: If an interview lasts longer than anticipated, don't be afraid to request time to make some calls to rearrange your schedule.

INFORMATIONAL INTERVIEW

1. Meeting scheduled by the job seeker with individuals presently working in jobs that appeal to job seeker or with individuals who hire for these jobs; not to interview for a specific position, but to explore the career field.

2. Offers job seekers the chance to gather information about what the job is really like, the opportunities, and required skills and education.

3. Crucial to prepare for the meeting by choosing questions that will give you information about the profession, enabling you to decide whether to pursue this career. Sample questions include:

    What are the greatest problems and challenges facing your industry?

    What skills, education, and experience are required for this job?

    How did you get to your current position?

    What are the most satisfying and most frustrating parts of your job?

4. Opportunity to confirm with interviewer whether you have the qualifications for the job and, if not, solicit suggestions on how you can better qualify.

5. Further your exploration by asking for names of additional contacts who can provide more information about opportunities in the field or industry.

Primary Interview Preparation—Know Thyself

Before you set foot on your first interview, take the time to truly know yourself. Explore and answer the following questions:

What position would give me the greatest satisfaction?

What are my interests, skills, and abilities?

What are my gifts, my greatest strengths?

List my five most significant accomplishments and why I am proud of them.

Why should an employer be interested in me?

What type of work situation and environment am I most comfortable in?

What are my short-term and long-range career plans?

What motivates and energizes me to do my best?

If you answer these questions honestly, they will not only point you to jobs that will give you pleasure, but help you analyze positions, their responsibilities, and organizations to determine if they will fulfill your short- and long-term occupational and career goals.

Tips on Preparing for an Interview

1. Most of us don't like surprises at an interview and you can avoid one if you ask with whom you will be meeting when scheduling your interview appointment. Check out the interviewer through your network, the organization's Web site, or research the individual through trade and professional journals.

Tip: Go out on the World Wide Web and conduct a search using the interviewer's name. You may locate all kinds of information to create targeted questions once you understand the interviewer and his or her background.

2. Contact your references and request permission to use them. You will need at minimum three professional references (ideally, individuals who can attest to your work performance). Prepare a reference sheet by centering your name, address, and phone number on an $8^1/_2 \times 11$-inch sheet of paper. Type and center the word "references" and follow with each reference's name, job title, organization name, business address, and home and business phone numbers. If a reference no longer works for the organization where he or she knew of your work, you can indicate "Former Controller" and on the next line state the organization for which he or she worked. You will take copies of this reference sheet with you on your interviews.

Tip: Fill your references in on what you are looking for and send them a copy of your current résumé so they can see what you have been up to.

3. Get directions to the location. Confirm the address, the building, and the floor or suite number. Inquire about parking facilities or accessibility to public transportation. Don't rely on the Internet to provide the directions; your contact will provide the most accurate directions based on the location and traffic at that time of day.

Tip: It's always helpful to take a dry run to unfamiliar locations.

4. Be on time. Many interviewers will not accept any excuse for lateness. Plan on getting to the location 15 minutes early—time to pull yourself together, but not long enough to get nervous.

5. Project the image of the position you are seeking. Appearance counts! If you are not sure of the dress code, check out the employees at lunch or quitting time. Don't take chances because inappropriate appearance may cost you the job. Find a professional style that is right for you. For more information on dress, see Chapter 16.

6. Thoroughly research the organization prior to the interview. Write a profile of the organization and develop a few questions based on your research. For information on how to research organizations and industries, see Chapter 15.

7. Familiarize yourself with the types of questions a potential employer can legally ask. Laws designed to protect you from discrimination also prohibit employers from asking questions that violate your civil rights. These laws are in effect for organizations that employ 15 or more workers. You do not have to answer questions related to your color, race, sex, religion, national origin, age, pregnancy, childbirth, or medical conditions. For an extensive listing of potential questions and answers, see Chapter 16.

8. Decide what skills, abilities, knowledge, and accomplishments you want to relate to the interviewer and rehearse your presentation. If

the line of questioning doesn't give you the opportunity to speak about these qualifications, take control of the interview. Achieve control by manipulating the answers to these questions by adding the information you would like the interviewer to have when making the hiring decision. Prior to the interview, carefully list what you have to offer the organization. Reveal details of your personal inventory throughout the interview.

9. Practice answering questions using a tape recorder. (Refer to Chapter 16 for tips on using a video camera.) Prepare a list of interview questions and ask a trusted friend or family member to act as the interviewer and ask the questions. Record the questions and answers and then play back the tape. Is your voice well modulated or shaky? Is there any hesitancy? How do your answers sound?

Tip: Critique your responses and then try again.

Continue to work until you hear improvements and feel confident in your voice and responses.

10. Prepare a closing statement that indicates your interest in the position. The interviewer lets you know the interview is ending by giving you a nonverbal signal, such as closing a pad, or telling you, "This will be my last question." Now is the time to convey interest. Whether or not you have expressed interest may make a difference in the final selection.

11. Bring extra copies of your résumé. The interviewer may not have a copy and there may be other individuals you will meet who should have a copy as well.

12. Consider purchasing a writing portfolio; it will hold your reference sheets and résumés and give you a place to rest your hands during the interview. Use the note pad to list the questions you'll ask; it is quite impressive to open the portfolio and reveal your prepared list when the interviewer asks if you have questions.

Special Situations

∾ *You are caught in an unavoidable traffic mishap.* Job seekers should invest in a cell phone—not to give your phone number to prospective employers but to have handy for communications in emergency situations. In this case, call ahead, apologize, be sincere, and explain the delay.

∾ *You know someone on the interview panel.* Ensure that you reveal the nature of the relationship prior to the interview. If a greeting is appropriate, it would be unusual not to recognize a friend or acquaintance. The panel will then be aware that a current or prior relationship exists and the other members will decide how to handle it.

∾ *The interviewer does all the talking and doesn't give you a chance to speak.* This is a frequent occurrence with inexperienced interviewers. Listen for a pause in the conversation and say "Mr. Miller, there are a few things I would like to tell you about myself and several questions I would like you to answer." When you follow up the interview with a thank-you letter, briefly state how your experience clearly relates to the job responsibilities.

∾ *The interviewer constantly lets phones and co-workers interrupt the interview.* Applicants should get the interviewer's full attention without interruptions. You may have inadvertently caught the interviewer in a crisis situation and you might say, "Excuse me, I see you are very busy. Would it be more convenient for you if we reschedule?" If this is not an emergency situation and the interviewer is rude, better to find this out in the exploration process.

∾ *You are requested to provide your current and unfriendly boss as a reference and this boss is the reason you are seeking a new job.* If you have not yet been offered a job, advise the prospective employer that once you have an offer, you will be happy to provide three professional references. If you have been offered a job and they would like your current boss as a reference, ask if it would be acceptable to use another manager in the organization who knows your work. If they question why, you can honestly offer the fact, without elaborating, that one of the reasons you are leaving the organization is because of your supervisor.

~ *You show up for the interview and are told the interviewer is sick and some-one else will substitute.* Clarify if the "substitute" has hiring authority or whether this will be a screening interview. If the substitute has hiring authority but will not be your supervisor, follow through with the interview but ask for a follow-up interview with the supervisor, even if you are offered a position.

Conducting Research for the Interview

15

Self-Test Your Savvy in Conducting Job Search Research:
Do You Know the Best Techniques for Locating Information
on Organizations and Industries?

The following self-test is a tool to help you assess whether you are ready to
conduct research. The objective is not to get the highest score possible, but to
pinpoint areas that you can strengthen to develop investigative skills to help
you discover information on organizations and industries that interest you.

1. The Internet is most effective for conducting research prior
   to the job interview.   T/F __
2. All branches in a library system have similar structure
   and resources.   T/F __
3. It's fairly easy to research companies that are publicly held.   T/F __
4. Privately owned companies are not listed on any stock
   exchange.   T/F __
5. It's very difficult to research government organizations.   T/F __
6. Public libraries are a great source for corporate information.   T/F __
7. You must own a computer to access the Internet.   T/F __
8. The Office of Public Liaison can provide information
   for federal agencies.   T/F __
9. All Internet search tools use the same search logic.   T/F __

10. By law, a publicly held corporation must report certain financial information to the Securities and Exchange Commission (SEC) and its shareholders.   T/F __

11. Anyone can borrow books and articles from public, college, university, and other library systems.   T/F __

12. The oldest subject-oriented search tool is Yahoo.   T/F __

13. Search engines are free-form research tools.   T/F __

14. You can use a company's stock or ticker symbol to help locate breaking company news.   T/F __

15. The Big Book is an Internet phone directory.   T/F __

16. Spiders and robots are computer programs found in search engines.   T/F __

17. Humans, not computers, catalog and index information for subject-oriented directories.   T/F __

18. One search engine will meet your Internet research needs.   T/F __

19. Public libraries have access to the Internet and database systems.   T/F __

20. Search tools on the Internet are free.   T/F __

Total: _____

Score 1 point for each "True" response and 0 for each "False" response, EXCEPT for questions 1, 2, 5, 7, 9, 18. *For these questions only*, **subtract** 1 point for each "True" response. Record your total. A score below +12 indicates that you would benefit from practicing the research techniques discussed in this chapter. (*Note:* It is possible to have a negative score.)

Research Fundamentals

Have you done enough research to know how you can fit into the organization? You'll need to identify basic information:

What the organization does

Its products and/or services

Its senior staff and officers

How long the company has been in business

How many subsidiaries it has

Its size

Its competition

How it ranks in its industry

Industry trends and projections

Leading companies in the industry

Corporate and industry problems and predictions concerning mergers, acquisitions, pending litigation, and bankruptcies

New technologies affecting the industry

Tips for Researching Organizations

The following ideas will help you thoroughly research an organization prior to your interview.

PRIVATE SECTOR

1. Determine if a company is publicly held (traded on a stock exchange), privately owned (not listed on any stock exchange), or a subsidiary of a publicly held organization.

2. By law, publicly held companies must report certain financial information to the Securities and Exchange Commission (SEC) and their shareholders.

3. Contact the company public relations department and request that an annual report (only available if it is publicly held) and any brochures, in-house newsletters, magazines, or promotional materials be sent to you by first-class mail. Or, you can arrange to pick them up. A corporation's own historian or information library may be able to supply additional information.

4. Identify corporate officers and top management through online and published directories. Use search engines and periodical indexes to locate newspaper and periodical articles by or about the company, its management, and industry.

Tip: Check the local newspaper where the organization is headquartered; if searching online, access its archives or back issues.

---

5. Use your contacts to locate current or past employees. They can supply firsthand information about the organization's dynamics.

PUBLIC SECTOR

1. Budgets for federal, state, and local governments are a matter of public record and are available for review online, in public libraries, and government offices.

2. Most public organizations produce in-house newsletters. Request copies as well as any other published literature through their public affairs office.

3. Contact the Office of Public Liaison at any federal government agency to see if it can send you fact sheets, which might include mission, history, authority, budget, type of work, programs, and additional activities.

4. Scan local newspapers and periodicals for articles on issues, budgets, board members, politicians, and government officials. Check periodical indexes for articles about the organization and its top management.

5. County and city governments often publish handbooks and profiles including extensive demographic information. Check with local government agencies or visit your local public library. Both usually keep copies of all published documents from local government.

Tip: Even telephone directories often include short histories and information about local government. Many public libraries have phone books from all over the United States.

Using the Library for Research

The library is a great source of information, despite our online dependency. But all libraries—even libraries belonging to the same system—are not the same. Not only do their sizes, budgets, staffs, and services differ, but they purchase different periodicals, directories, and materials for their collections.

Regional, large public, and college and university libraries have the most extensive collections, including business and general periodical indexes, business and technical journals, and newspapers.

There are also specialized libraries found at professional and trade associations. Even your local newspaper may have a library open to the public.

The interlibrary loan system allows most libraries throughout the United States to borrow books and articles for you from public, college, university, and other libraries. You supply the specific titles of books and articles you want, and your local library makes the arrangements. As part of the service, materials can also be photocopied for a small fee. Check your library for the maximum number of requests allowed and any fees. The service takes a couple of weeks, so you'll have to use some other means if you are in a hurry.

Many libraries have access to database systems and the Internet. They will perform searches for you for free or for a small fee, depending on the complexity of your search.

SELECTED CORPORATE DIRECTORIES

Directory of Corporate Affiliations
National Register Publishing Company

In-depth view of over 18,000 public and private businesses and their divisions, subsidiaries, and affiliates in the U.S. and throughout the world with revenues in excess of $10 million or workforce in excess of 300. Lists non-U.S.-based companies with revenues in excess of $50 million. Includes index of mergers, acquisitions, and name changes. Updated annually.

Thomas Register
Thomas Publishing Company
www.thomasregister.com

A 33-volume set with a company profiles section that lists more than 156,000 U.S. companies including: corporate addresses, phone numbers, asset ratings, company executives, locations of sales offices, plants, and some subsidiary/division and product line information. Annually updated.

Hoover's Handbook of American Business
Hoover's Handbook of Emerging Companies
Hoover's Handbook of World Business
Hoover's Handbook of Private Companies
www.hoovers.com

Four-title series of handbooks. Covers the biggest, fastest-growing, and most influential enterprises in the world. Updated annually.

Million Dollar Directory
Dun and Bradstreet, Inc.

Includes information on 160,000 U.S. businesses with $9 million or more in sales volume. Updated annually.

Standard and Poor's Register of Corporations, Directors, and Executives

Standard and Poor's Corporation

Lists over 75,000 profiles of U.S. and Canadian corporations and provides names and titles of 437,500 executives and 71,000 biographical sketches of top-level managers.

Standard and Poor's Corporation Records

Standard and Poor's Corporation

Short history, financial information, and description of various publicly and privately held corporations.

SELECTED GENERAL DIRECTORIES

Encyclopedia of Associations

The Gale Group

Lists 23,000 national and international organizations including trade, business, commercial, environmental and agricultural, legal, government, public administration, military, engineer, technological, national and social sciences, education, cultural, social welfare, health and medical, public affairs, fraternal, nationality, ethnic, religious, veterans, hobby, avocational, athletics and sports, labor unions, associations and federations, chambers of commerce, trade and tourism, Greek letter.

The Standard Periodical Directory

Oxbridge Communications
info@mediafinder.com

Single-volume source of comprehensive information on U.S. and Canadian periodical publications with 248 subject categories.

SELECTED PUBLIC SECTOR DIRECTORIES

World Chamber of Commerce Directory

worldchamberdirectory@compuserve.com

Includes State Chambers of Commerce, U.S. Chambers of Commerce, Economic Development organizations, Canadian Chambers of Commerce, foreign Chambers of Commerce. Updated annually in June.

Washington 2000

Columbia Books, Inc.

www.columbiabooks.com

A comprehensive directory of the area's major institutions and the people who run them, including national government, local government, international affairs, national affairs, the media, business, national associations, labor unions, the bar, medical and health foundations and philanthropy, science and political research, education, religious and cultural institutions, clubs, community affairs. Updated annually.

Washington Information Directory

Congressional Quarterly Inc.

Easy-to-use source of details on federal government departments and agencies, the U.S. Congress, and nonprofit organizations. Information of state government officials and diplomats. Updated annually.

The U.S. Government Manual

U.S. Government Printing Office

Provides comprehensive information on agencies of the legislative, judicial, and executive branches; quasi-official agencies; international organizations in which U.S. participates; boards; commissions; and committees.

Using the Internet for Research

There are millions of Web sites on the Internet that contain an unfathomable amount of information. The Internet can truly be your partner in all phases of the job search. It's used most often to prepare job seekers for the interview, but it can also help you screen organizations and select potential matches before you even send out your résumé or schedule an interview. You'll have this world of information available at your fingertips if you learn how to search.

Unfortunately, the Internet does not resemble a traditional library where everything falls neatly into a subject area index format. You'll need to rely on two search tools to locate information: subject-oriented directories and search engines.

There is no single search tool that offers a comprehensive index of Internet sites and there are numerous choices within each search type. Savvy job seekers use a combination of search tools to find the best source of information based on their specific needs. All of the search tools are free to job seekers connected to the Internet.

Tip: If you don't have a computer or access to the Internet, use your public library. Most libraries now have public Internet stations where you can conduct your online research. Remember, all you need to use these tools is access to the Internet; there are no additional fees. These powerful research tools are free to users because they are supported by advertisers or sponsors.

Subject-Oriented Directories

The subject-oriented directory contains a database of sites. For those unfamiliar with online searching, subject-oriented directories are easy to use. It's also a quick way to find general information on the Internet. As their name implies, subject-oriented directories organize information in a hierarchical or catalog format starting with broad headings and working down to more specific categories. These search tools are managed by a cadre of human cataloguers or indexers. Because they rely on human intervention, the total size of their database of sites is limited, and the dynamic nature of the Internet makes them high-maintenance sites. But they represent an excellent resource for targeted general information because their sites are "hand picked." When you search a subject-oriented directory, you are not searching the entire Internet, only the database of sites of that particular directory.

SELECTED SUBJECT-ORIENTED DIRECTORIES

Yahoo (www.yahoo.com), the oldest and most widely known subject-oriented search tool, is a subject-tree style catalogue that organizes the Web into 14 major topics: Arts, Business and Economy, Computers and Internet, Education, Entertainment, Government, Health, News, Recreation, Reference, Regional, Science, Social Science, and Society and Culture. Within each topic is a list of subtopics, and under each of those is another list, and another, and so on, moving from the more general to the more specific.

Other popular subject-oriented guides are **Look Smart (www.look smart.com)** and **Snap (www.snap.com)**. They have a similar structure, but each guide has a different database of sites.

Tip: Use several guides to increase your chances of finding useful information.

SEARCH TIPS FOR SUBJECT-ORIENTED DIRECTORIES

There are several ways you can use a subject-oriented directory in your job search. For example:

- STEP 1: Go to the Yahoo Web site at www.yahoo.com.
- STEP 2: Select the "Business and Economy" category.
- STEP 3: From the next menu select "Employment and Work" and then select "Yahoo Careers."
- STEP 4: One of the categories of the Yahoo Careers Section is Research. In the Research section you will find more specific sections devoted to Industry Research, Company Profiles, Salaries and Benefits, and Advice.
- STEP 5: From there you can look at an industry, find profiles of many publicly traded companies, and locate salary and benefit information.

The next way to search for information would be to use the dialogue box found on Yahoo's main page at www.yahoo.com. For example:

- STEP 1: Enter the "Company Profiles" in the dialogue box and click on the "Search" button. The result will be six category matches as well as one Inside Yahoo match.
- STEP 2: Select the "Company Profiles" match and you will find links to Forbes 500, Fortune 500, and Inc. 500 as well as other sites.
- STEP 3: Click on "Company Profiles" from the Inside Yahoo section, and you will find company profiles from Market Guide. They provide users with information on over 9,000 public companies, including contact information, business summaries, officer and employee information, sector and industry classifications, business and earnings announcement summaries, and financial statistics and ratios. The information found in these pages can help you prepare for the interview and provide information to compose targeted questions.

Search Engines

Search engines are high-powered free-form research tools that rely on software technology. Computer programs, known as spiders or robots, search the Internet and add or modify sites in their database. The common goal of all search engines is to index as much of the Web as possible. Search engines have a query or dialogue box where you enter your search terms. Some search engines may also offer subject guides based on their popularity and ease of use. However, the true power of these tools lies in the free-form query.

Search engines look for a match for your query based on hypertext markup language or HTML, the underlying code used to create all Web pages. They'll generate a ranked list of sites that match your query as closely as possible.

Each search engine uses a unique type of logic such as Boolean, natural language, or phrase searching. It is important to understand the logic that a search engine uses in order to phrase your query in such a way that it will find the information you are looking for. Use the HELP feature and become familiar with the search engine logic before using any of these tools.

No single search engine provides a comprehensive search of the Internet, but a combination of search engines will help you find what you are looking for.

FIVE SEARCH ENGINES—AND HOW TO USE THEM

1. **Altavista (www.altavista.com)**, developed by Digital Equipment Corporation as a prototype, is one of the largest and most comprehensive search engines. You can search either by word, phrase, or question. A powerful feature is the ability to limit a search to a specific Internet domain. For example, if you are looking for information on a nonprofit organization, enter the organization name in the search dialogue box followed by "host:org." Altavista will search its database for all matches within the .org Internet domain.

2. **Ask Jeeves (www.ask.com)** uses natural language query in the form of a question, a technology used by other search engines. Ask a question like: "Where can I find company profiles?" and this combination search engine and meta-search engine provides a list of relevant sites including Hoovers Online, Yahoo Business, and other resources.

3. **Fast Search (www.alltheweb.com)** provides access to a large database of sites in a very efficient manner. Its trademark "All the Web, All the Time" says it all. You'll get a ranked list of sites matching your query as well as the elapsed time for the search in milliseconds. The dialogue box search options include "all the words," "any of the words," or "the exact phrase."

4. **Google (www.google.com)** uses advanced search techniques to generate targeted results for your query. The hyper-search technology recognizes sites as hubs (groups of links) and authorities on particular topics. Results are delivered in order of importance and relevance.

5. **Hotbot (www.hotbot.com)** lets you put date limits on your search to filter out the most recently updated Web sites. You can narrow your request to sites that have been updated as recently as the last two weeks or as long ago as two years.

Digital Libraries

Digital libraries or virtual libraries represent the Internet version of public libraries. These online catalogs seek to emulate and extend traditional libraries by organizing their collections into categories along the lines of recognized indexing and cataloging systems. Librarians are typically information-organization experts, so you should find these sources particularly helpful.

THREE DIGITAL LIBRARIES—AND WHAT THEY OFFER

1. **Argus Clearinghouse (www.clearinghouse.net)** provides a selective collection of topical guides. The "Business and Employment" category has guides on diverse commercial enterprise topics including, but not limited to, products, trade, markets, financial matters, professions, and job seeking. Go to the "Business" category and then select the "Companies" sub category for links to company information and business research.
2. **Internet Public Library (www.ipl.org)** is the first Internet public library. Go to the "Reference" section and look in the "Business and Economics" category. The "Business Directories" or "Employment" sub categories have links to company-related information.
3. **The Virtual Library (www.vlib.org)** is the oldest catalog of the Web created by Tim Berners-Lee, the inventor of the World Wide Web. Go to the "Business and Economics" section and look in the "Finance" category. Click on the "Business Job Finder" and you will connect to the "Careers in Business" section of the site.

Twelve Top Web Sites for Researching Companies and Industries

- **American Companies (www.americancompanies.com)** lists U.S. *Fortune* 500 companies by location and industry.

- **Corporate Information (www.corporateinformation.com)** is a financial portal with over 300,000 company profiles, public company profiles, research reports, and links to other sites.

- **Edgar Online (www.edgar-online.com)** provides access to Securities and Exchange Commission filings for publicly traded corporations.

- **Employer Profiles (www.company.monster.com)** lists company profiles in alphabetical order or by state.

- **Forbes (www.forbes.com)** includes information on the top 500 private companies organized by industry, rank, or alphabetical order.

- **Hoovers Online (www.hoovers.com)** provides databases of company profiles, a weekly industry profile, and company news.

- **Inc. 500 (www.inc.com)** details the companies selected by *Inc.* magazine as the fastest-growing private companies in the United States.

- **JobFind Corporate Profiles (www.jobfind.com)** provides a pull-down menu to select a company and its history, employee benefits, corporate philosophy, and culture.

- **WashingtonJobs.com (www.washingtonjobs.com)** from the *Washington Post* Online provides links to job resources and trade directories for researching companies and industries.

- **Careers.WSJ.com (www.careers.wsj.com)**, from the publishers of the *Wall Street Journal*, includes links to who's hiring, company profiles, salary surveys, and other career-related information.

- **Occupational Outlook Handbook (www.bls.gov/ocohome.htm)** is a nationally recognized source of career information, designed to provide valuable assistance to individuals making decisions about their future work lives. Revised every two years, the *Handbook* describes what workers do on the job, working conditions, the training and education needed, earnings, and expected job prospects in a wide range of occupations.

- **Career Guide to Industries (www.bls.gov/cghome.htm)** from the U.S. Department of Labor, Bureau of Labor Statistics is a companion to the *Occupational Outlook Handbook*. It details over 42 industries, providing information on available careers by industry, including the nature of the industry, working conditions, employment, occupations in the industry, training and advancement, earnings and benefits, employment outlook, and lists of organizations that offer additional information.

Tips for Researching Companies on the Internet

1. Publicly held companies will most likely have a Web site and volumes of information because they must disclose financial data to shareholders and the Securities and Exchange Commission.
2. Use the company's stock or ticker symbol to help locate breaking company news. Use this to research the financial condition of the company or current news on products, services, pending litigation, or other important information that will help you develop targeted questions for the interview.
3. Newspapers are a wonderful source of company information. Look for newspapers online at American Journalism Review (www.ajr. newslink.org).
4. Trade associations provide background information and sources for industries. Use the Dow Jones Business Directory (www.bd. dowjones.com) for reviews of major industry Web sites, business profiles, and news.
5. Internet phone directories have basic contact information such as phone number and address. Two standard references are the Big Book (www.bigbook.com) and Big Yellow (www.bigyellow.com).
6. Financial Web sites are plentiful and they're helpful for locating company profiles. Use the databases at Finance Web (www. finweb.com).
7. Follow business news by using online business publications. Find recent news sources at Business Wire (www.businesswire.com) and PR News Wire (www.prnewswire.com). Business Wire and PR News Wire provide one week's worth of business news from a variety of sources. Check these sites for last-minute or breaking news information prior to your interview.
8. Research markets and industries through Hoover's Industry Zone (www.hoovers.com). It profiles 25 separate industry sectors, a useful

resource to learn more about a specific industry before narrowing down prospective employers.

9. There is such a vast amount of information out there, you may have difficulty locating exactly what you are seeking. Meta-information, information about information, may solve your needs. If you can at least find the Web site for a potential employer, you will most likely find an e-mail contact point. Use the e-mail contact to request more information about the company. Your timing may provide you with hidden job opportunities that have not yet been advertised.

10. Try the following when you've exhausted all resources to locate a company's Web site. In the location or address dialogue box of your browser (Netscape or Microsoft Internet Explorer), type in "www." followed by the company's name; then type in ".com" after the name. If the company has a Web site it will more than likely incorporate its name. For example, if you were seeking employment with a company called "My Company," type "www.mycompany.com" in your browser and it will usually bring up the corporate Web site. If you are looking for a nonprofit organization, just replace the ".com" with ".org."

Communicating Your Qualifications

16

Self-Test Your Savvy in Using Verbal and Nonverbal Communications in the Interview: How Good Are You at Communicating in Person?

The following self-test is a tool to help you assess whether you are ready to participate in the interview process. The objective is not to get the highest score possible, but to pinpoint areas that you can strengthen to develop persuasive verbal and nonverbal communication skills that will help you demonstrate how your qualifications fit a job's requirements.

1. I should not ask the interviewer any questions until he or she has asked me if I have any questions.   T/F __
2. Pauses are okay. Both the interviewer and I need them for reflection.   T/F __
3. I may be asked and need not answer "What does your spouse do?"   T/F __
4. I will be evaluated on my appearance and poise as well as my experience and education.   T/F __
5. Applicants who avoid eye contact are thought to have something to hide.   T/F __
6. I may be asked and should answer "What is your social security number?"   T/F __

7. It's important to be relaxed, so I should sit in whatever way makes me feel comfortable. T/F __

8. I should appear enthusiastic at all times. T/F __

9. Be wary of any extremes in dress. T/F __

10. It's okay to take time to formulate my answers. T/F __

11. I should be able to figure out the questions without asking for clarification. T/F __

12. I may be asked and need not answer "Are you a United States citizen?" T/F __

13. I should dress slightly conservatively to be on the safe side. T/F __

14. If someone asks me my weaknesses, I should be honest and say I sometimes have trouble meeting deadlines. T/F __

15. I should prepare specific questions for every interview. T/F __

16. I read somewhere that I shouldn't wear something brand new to the interview. T/F __

17. I may be asked and need not answer "How tall are you?" T/F __

18. When asked a question, I should determine what the interviewer is trying to learn about me. T/F __

19. I should never criticize a past employer. T/F __

20. I should beware of asking questions that imply that I have the job. T/F __

21. I must account for gaps in employment. T/F __

22. It's important to use a close, whether interested in the position or not. T/F __

Total: _____

Score 1 point for each "True" response and 0 for each "False" response, EXCEPT for questions 1, 7, 11, 14, 22. *For these questions only*, **subtract** 1 point for each "True" response. Record your total. A score below +15 indicates that you would benefit from practicing the interview techniques discussed in this chapter. (*Note:* It is possible to have a negative score.)

Question Fundamentals

An interviewer wants to select the candidate who best meets the job requirements. The questions he or she asks will be formulated to determine whether you have the necessary qualifications.

Applicants who calmly and capably detail their credentials are more likely to make a positive interview impression. Most job seekers can talk about themselves comfortably if they're well prepared. Provide the interviewer with information that makes it easier to assess your credentials.

Promote Yourself with a Two-Minute Summary

You'll gain confidence and control if you prepare a two-minute summary that articulates highlights of your experience, background, education, training, and accomplishments. But the summary only works if it's a natural statement from the heart that flows easily. The two-minute summary is:

- Used as a marketing tool
- An easy way to communicate your qualifications and demonstrate proficiency
- Delivered in its entirety
- Broken into components you can integrate throughout the interview

Each applicant is unique and your summary must demonstrate what is special about you. It should be on a professional level, but it is permissible to include some personal information that distinguishes you from other applicants.

Tip: Always bear in mind that the purpose of the interview is to demonstrate how your qualifications meet job requirements; only include information that makes you a more viable candidate.

Choose from the following selected topics:

- *Personal characteristics or traits* that developed your interests, abilities, direction, or motivation; for example, the geographic area or town where you grew up, birth order, family member career influence, or teacher mentor. *Example:* "I am the youngest of six and knew from an early age that I would need to move away to distinguish myself. New York University offered a wonderful graphic arts program and the opportunity to build a life in a different part of the country."

- *Education or specialized training;* for example, college, university, internships, or certification or diploma programs. *Example:* "I've had a life-long passion for anything mechanical. I have enjoyed working with personal computers and decided to pursue the MCSE designation. I enjoyed the program and would like to apply these skills in a systems analyst position."

- *Life experience* that has defined your character, qualities, or career choices, such as financing your college education, changing career course due to family events, relocating many times, or living or studying overseas. *Example:* "My father died when I was 11 and it was impossible for my mom to pay for my college education. I took a variety of jobs during school vacations and while attending college. It was difficult but I developed an extraordinary strength and focus. I apply those qualities to every experience and find I consistently accomplish whatever goal I choose."

- *Work history* from actual experiences, progression, mentors, industry, or organizations. *Example:* "I began my career in the credit control function and realized after six years that I really wanted to pursue a financial accounting career. I went back to college part-time and completed a Master of Science in Accounting. After exploring many options I began working as an auditor and have progressed from audit manager to audit director. This field is an exact match for my knowledge, skills, abilities, and interests."

- *Career goals* demonstrated by short- and long-term goals and possibly the reasons why you have chosen this particular path. *Example:* "I began my career in catering sales at a luxury hotel. I enjoyed the sales aspect but wanted a different customer base so I switched industries a year ago to sell pharmaceuticals to health-care professionals. While working as a sales representative for Company ABC, I qualified as a President's Club winner and won an all-expenses paid trip to the Caribbean for achieving 110% of plan. My next goal is to enroll in an Executive MBA program and use those credentials to pursue a District Sales Manager opportunity within the pharmaceutical industry."

- *Accomplishments* related to career goals, job-specific, industry, community, or professional affiliations. Any awards or recognitions based on performance or contributions. *Example:* "I taught an introductory course for customer service and prepared massive handouts because I couldn't locate a book I really liked to use with the curriculum. The course was very successful and the participants asked for more handouts. I was an English major in college and always wanted to write a book so I thought I would write and self-publish a book for the course. I located a small publisher who was willing to publish it. The book has been well received and has sold over 10,000 copies; a true fulfillment of my life-long dream."

Tip: Draft your summary as either a narrative, sentences, or bullets. Practice your summary until you can comfortably share it in a conversational tone because it loses its impact if read from notes.

Twelve Frequently Asked Interview Questions— and How to Respond

Don't let interview questions unnerve you. When crafting answers to questions, don't panic; ask yourself, "What is the interviewer trying to learn about me?" It is easier to respond to questions when you understand why the question is being asked.

1. **"Tell me about yourself."** While intimidating at first, this is a very common question that you should master. Make the question work in your favor by controlling what you tell the interviewer, revealing as much about yourself as you'd like. The interviewer does not want to hear your life history, but rather, pertinent facts about your qualifications (e.g., experience and training) and any details that demonstrate your interest and knowledge of the position, industry, and

your career progress. This is a perfect place to use your two-minute summary. Practice until you have your response down pat.

2. **"What are your strengths?"** The interviewer wants to know what is unique about you. Where's your expertise, specialty, best skill, or the key to your success? Choose two to three strengths, usually skills or abilities, that you can elaborate on how you developed, when you apply, or what's so special. Frequent responses run the gamut from communication, interpersonal, organizational, and troubleshooting skills to analytical or technical abilities.

Tip: One interviewee was very disturbed when asked "What would you like written on your tombstone?" Try to determine what the interviewer is trying to learn about you. In this case, how would you like to be remembered or what is special about you? A proper response would be similar to that used for "What are your strengths?"

---

3. **"What are your weaknesses?"** This question often follows "What are your strengths?" While the interviewer may be very interested in your tardiness or inability to make deadlines, this is not the time to bare your soul. Think of a potential weakness that is really a strength or a mild weakness that you have already made strides in improving. For example, "I am a perfectionist and I find it hard to empathize with colleagues who are not so committed to achieving top performance. But, I realize this is a weakness and I have been working hard at not holding others up to my standards." Or, "Technology and the workplace have been changing so rapidly that I find it hard to plan my career much further than a year. I would like to do some research and establish a five-year plan and hope the next organization encourages this process."

4. **"Where do you expect to be in five years?"** In the best of all worlds it is important that you plan your career, identifying positions of interest and acquiring skills, training, and experience to position yourself for progressive moves. If possible, do your homework so you can answer this question accurately. Or, tell the interviewer the position you are seeking, your desire to establish a long-term relationship with the organization, and interest in planning career goals.

5. **"How is your previous experience applicable to the work we do here?"** First, you need a good grasp of the work they do and this is where your research comes into play. The most desirable candidates match their experience to the needs and plans of the organization. Good preparation is important prior to each interview; not just how to answer generic questions, but how your qualifications relate to that specific employer and its job openings.

Tip: If you were unable to perform adequate research or the interview came up suddenly, query the interviewer about the organization and its goals so you can match your qualifications to its needs.

6. **"Why are you leaving your present position?"** Most people leave their jobs because they are bored, unchallenged, lack growth, or are dissatisfied with the organization or their supervisor. The best response to this question is "lack of challenge" or "lack of opportunity to advance" and be prepared to tell the interviewer just what challenge or opportunity you seek.

    Should you relay that you have been terminated or laid off? Human resource experts say you should be honest because this information will frequently surface during a reference check. If the layoff was legitimate, you should still be able to provide a supervisory reference for that organization. Frame your response as positively as you can, such as: "Yes, I was laid off along with my whole department in a restructuring and no other positions were available for us" or "I had requested the first shift and I was informed that if no opportunity was available, I would be asked to find another position."

    If you don't reveal that you have been terminated, human resource experts say the discrepancy will probably be discovered during reference checks and the hiring manager will not feel so good about the hire.

7. **"What salary are you looking for?"** The best way to answer a question about salary is with a question. When asked this question, counter with "What salary are you offering?" If the interviewer shoots back another question (he or she can be as savvy as you), ask "Can you tell me the salary range?" If you run out of questions and

seem to get no hint of the proposed salary, you can tell the interviewer you are interested in the same salary range quoted in the (provide an industry, association, or government salary study for your occupation) salary survey. Try not to give an exact amount; if you do, it is quite common to find you undervalued yourself and you may find out later that you could have started with a higher salary.

Tip: Do research salary ranges for your occupation and industry prior to your interview and have a good grasp of your worth in the marketplace. For information on researching salaries, see Chapter 17.

8. **"Why do you want to work here?"** Why are you interested in the organization? Have you been impressed with online and media articles about the organization, products, or projects? Do you have former colleagues, friends, or family who either work there or know of someone who does who thinks highly of the organization? The interviewer is looking for substance—that you not only know something about them but have great interest in becoming a member of their team.

9. **"Why does this job interest you?"** What is most appealing about the position? The research, writing, media relations, sales, or technical skills you'll use? The work team, corporate or office environment, clients, equipment, or career growth and opportunity? Persuade the interviewer why you and the position are a good match.

10. **"To date, what have been your two most important career accomplishments?"** Choose several career accomplishments that give you great pride and from these, identify why they are important to you. Was it the difficulty in achieving your goal, obstacles you overcame, team effort involved, or organizational gains based on your efforts? Use this question to reveal your strong points and you'll elaborate on your values and strengths.

11. **"What will your former supervisors say about you?"** Take a positive approach, providing favorable written and verbal comments from current and prior supervisors. Or, address your strengths and accomplishments in performing your responsibilities. Honesty is the best policy; your comments may be verified through a reference check.

12. **"Why should we hire you?"** Tell the interviewer why you are the best person for the job; if you don't, the next candidate will! Employers are looking for employees who are confident in their qualifications and know that their performance can make a difference. Once again, demonstrate how you can help the organization meet its goals.

Tip: When discussing the position, align yourself with the employer by using the word "we"; for example, "we could solve that problem by . . ." or "we can compete more effectively with a marketing and sales team approach . . ."

Thirteen Stress Questions—and How to Respond

Interviewers ask stress questions to see how you handle pressure and yourself in less than optimal situations. Compose answers that are truthful, but use caution in providing negative information or circumstances; it will only make you look bad.

1. **"Tell me about a work experience that didn't work out."** Choose an experience that doesn't cast you in an unfavorable light and explain what you learned from it.
2. **"Would you describe an instance where your work was criticized."** Share an experience and describe how you used the information to improve your performance.
3. **"In your present position, what problems have you identified that had been previously overlooked?"** Select an accomplishment and describe how you identified the problem and your final resolution. Be wary of words and tone that portray your organization or predecessor in a negative manner.
4. **"Have you terminated staff before?"** Answer truthfully but be prepared to justify your decision and process.
5. **"Are you a good manager?"** It's important to provide an honest assessment of your managerial style, philosophy, and performance. You can relay comments from subordinates and supervisory evaluations.
6. **"How would you evaluate your present organization?"** Chances are you wouldn't be looking elsewhere if you were fully satisfied with

your present organization, but beware of venting your frustrations in the interview. Find something to praise and, if necessary, share the lack of mobility, challenge, career progression, or reduction in staff that is prompting your job search.

7. **"What didn't you like about your last supervisor?"** Be very tactful in answering this question. Identify a generic quality that combines the strength and weakness response. For example: "My supervisor was so conscientious and involved in his work that there was rarely time for staff directives" or "My supervisor had a relentless travel schedule and I had very little time to work with her on organizational goals."

8. **"Tell me about a complex problem you had to deal with."** This is a wonderful opportunity to share how you solve problems. Take a complicated example and break down how you approached the resolution and the end result.

9. **"Can you tell me how you resolved a difficult experience with a client?"** Select a problem that you successfully solved and detail the process you followed to improve communications and resolve difficulties.

10. **"How would you define a conducive work environment?"** The interviewer would like to know what kind of work environment inspires you to peak performance.

11. **"What frustrates you the most?"** This question could be another version of the weakness question. Identify a frustration that you are correcting to improve your performance. For example: "I find paperwork bottlenecks frustrating so I take the initiative to identify the quickest process and follow it through to implementation."

12. **"I don't think your background meets our requirements. Do you agree? If not, please explain."** Calmly and politely point out those qualifications that you feel are important and ask the interviewer if that changes his or her opinion. You might ask the interviewer to disclose any discrepancies between the selection criteria and your qualifications and then summarize how you feel your credentials match the job requirements.

13. **"Is there anything you would like to tell us that we have not covered in the interview?"** This might be a good time to restate

either your interest in the position or why you would be a good hire. One applicant stated: "No one who has ever hired me has been sorry."

What to Say in an Interview

Don't wait for the "right questions" so you can detail your credentials. Identify in advance what qualities make you uniquely qualified for the position and do not leave the interview until you have shared this information. Consider:

1. How your experience parallels the job requirements
2. Key accomplishments
3. Industry knowledge
4. Applicable and/or transferrable skills
5. Specialized training and/or education
6. How you can make a difference

What Not to Say in an Interview

A good interviewer makes you feel comfortable and establishes a cordial environment to discuss your background and qualifications. Do not be misled in thinking this person is on your side and you can share "anything" without consequences. The interviewer's goal is to weed out applicants who may not be the right fit. Negative statements will cost you opportunities. *Avoid:*

1. Statements that make you appear desperate. In response to "Why should we hire you?" for example, do not respond "Because I really need the job."
2. Responses that indicate previous job difficulties. If you've had any personality conflicts, no matter if you truly were not at fault, do not share the information with the interviewer.
3. Facts about your personal life.
4. Details that reveal information that may lead to discrimination or bias. You are protected by laws that prohibit discrimination based on your race, color, national origin, sex, religion, age, and disabilities, and it is illegal for employers to solicit this information.

in an Interview

A successful interview requires participation from you as well as from the interviewer. The more you participate, the more favorable the interview.

Tip: Always be prepared to ask questions because if you don't, you will appear to lack curiosity.

An interview is not an interrogation but a two-way street. You need to conduct your own interview, asking questions that will help you determine if the position and the organization are the right fit.

The interviewer plans questions and so must you. Spend some time prior to the interview jotting down your questions about the job and the organization. Develop a few questions based on your research that demonstrate knowledge of the organization. Look at industry trends and opportunities. For example:

"I read in the *Wall Street Journal* that you're planning to merge with XYZ Company. How does the marketing department fit into this new structure?"

"Will you be developing a new long-distance service now that XXY has introduced one?"

"In what direction do you see your organization going if the government passes the new bill on growth restrictions?"

Add any of the following questions to your list:

1. "What qualities are you looking for in candidates for this position?"

Tip: Listen carefully to this response and use the information throughout the interview to detail how your qualifications match the requirements.

---

2. "Is this a new position or a replacement? If a replacement, why?"

Tip: If you want to ask what happened to your predecessor, ask: "How many employees have had this position in the last four years?" "Why are the former employees no longer in the position?" "How many employees have been promoted from this position in the last four years?"

---

3. "What is the biggest challenge in this job from your perspective?"
4. "What is the company's retention rate and how do you keep up employee morale?"
5. "What strategic direction is this organization taking over the next five years?"
6. "What do you enjoy most about working here?"
7. "Please give me a profile of the employees here; for example, average age, gender mix, educational backgrounds."
8. "How does the organization handle problem-solving?"
9. "What kind of supervision will I have?"

   If you are very interested in the position and comfortable in an assertive role, include one of the following questions:

10. "I think the position is a good fit for me. What do you think?"
11. "I hope I am one of the candidates you are considering. When will you make a decision?" Or, "When may I expect to hear from you?"
12. "I am very interested. Are you considering me?"

in an Interview

There is certain information that you need to know prior to making an employment decision. For example: "How much vacation, holiday, or sick time will I get?" But usually the time to ask these questions is after you have received a job offer.

The following questions shouldn't be asked during a job interview, as they may make the interviewer question your priorities.

1. "How long is the lunch hour?"
2. "Are people easy to get along with here?"
3. "Where will my office be?"
4. Personal questions about the interviewer—such as education or experience; for example, "Have you ever been laid off?"
5. Any question that puts the interviewer on the spot; for example, "Does your company permit dating among employees?"
6. Questions that imply you don't know much about the organization and haven't done your homework; for example, "I noticed you are building a larger facility. Which area are you expanding?"

Isn't It Against the Law?

Employers are required by law to only ask interview questions that will reveal how well you might be expected to perform in a position. Laws and regulations govern the selection process and protect you from unfair discrimination in employment based on race, religion, sex, age, national origin, ethnicity, and disability.

You should not be asked questions related to:

> age or your date of birth
>
> arrest record
>
> citizenship or national origin
>
> credit or garnishment records
>
> personal information such as your plans to have a family, the number and ages of children, or child-care arrangements
>
> marital status or maiden name
>
> health history
>
> political or religious affiliations

Twelve Interview Questions You Need Not Answer

1. "We have a young staff. Because of your age, will you have trouble relating to young people?"
2. "Have you ever been arrested?"
3. "What does your spouse do?"
4. "I can't place your accent. What country are you from?"
5. "What is your marital status?"
6. "Do you own your own home?"
7. "What arrangements have you made to care for your children?"
8. "Do you plan to have children?"
9. "Do you have any physical disabilities?"
10. "How is your health?"
11. "Are you a Democrat?"
12. "Do you belong to a church?"

Special Situations

〜 *You are asked a question and have no idea how to answer it.* You can change the subject by volunteering different information or be candid and state that you have no experience in that area. An honest response, "That is a question I did not anticipate. May I think it over and get back to you?" may work or, if the question is crucial to the job function, it make knock you out of the running.

〜 *You are asked an inappropriate question, clearly a question that is illegal to ask.* How you feel about the question or the information that it will reveal should determine your response. Gauge how offensive the question is, how well the interview is going, and your comfort level in responding. If someone asks "How old are you anyway?" you could reply "That's an interesting question. Does age have any bearing on the performance for this job?" Or, you could smile and say, "I'm old enough to know that question isn't a proper question." If the question offends you or could lead to a discriminatory decision, carefully try to redirect the line of questioning. Or, reply "I prefer not to answer that question but will answer any questions relating to the job's duties."

〜 *You realize after a short time that you don't want the job.* Honestly state that after hearing the details of the position, you realize it would not meet your career goals. If you are still interested in the organization, let the interviewer know that and request your résumé be kept on file should another position open that would utilize your experience.

〜 *The interviewer asks you partway through the interview if you would be interested in a different position.* The interviewer may be testing you to determine your commitment to the position, may truly be exploring a better fit for your talents, or a job opening just occurred. If you are fully committed to the position under discussion, state this. Or, ask for full details of the other position and, if interested, request the opportunity to consider both options.

〜 *You are interviewing for an internal job; another position within your organization.* The interview follows the same basic principles with a few differences. While it is not okay to use buzz words and phrases that only have meaning within your organization on an external interview, it is perfectly fine and preferable to use them to describe your background and qualifications when interviewing internally. It's always prudent to use caution in describing your boss but even more so if the interview is internal and the interviewer may have knowledge of or know your supervisor.

~ *The interviewer questions your reliability because you've held three positions with three different employers in the past four years.* You must be prepared to deal with this question if you've had frequent job changes. Detail your career goals and job interests and explain that the organizations and positions were not what you anticipated and did not fit these objectives. Use this as an opportunity to discuss in depth the organization's plans, the job responsibilities, and your qualifications. Set yourself a personal goal to thoroughly evaluate an organization and position before making another commitment.

~ *You just enter your home and the phone rings. It is a hiring manager wanting to conduct a telephone interview.* Many organizations screen applicants by telephone to save time and recruitment costs and it is in your best interest to be prepared should you be contacted. But if the call comes at an inopportune time and you are uncomfortable, ask if you may call back. If you do take the call, it will potentially indicate a level of confidence not shown by other candidates.

~ *You are not offered the job.* If you were really interested in the position or the organization, call back and ask what additional qualifications you should acquire or what you could do better to get the next job.

Words to Use in an Interview

accessible	dedicated	energized	go-getter
achieved	dependable	enthusiastic	hard-working
accurate	doer	ethical	hire
adaptable	diligent	facilitated	honest
ambitious	driven	facilitator	initiative
clinched	eager	flexible	initiator
committed	effective	fulfilled	innovative
competent	empathetic	gained	instrumental

leader	productive	rectified	transformed
motivated	promoted	revamped	trustworthy
open	qualified	revived	upgraded
patient	quick	saved	versed
proactive	rebuilt	stimulated	willing
producer	receptive	trailblazer	

Three Verbs to Use in the Interview Along With "I"

I can—implies you will be able to or know how to

I will—implies your willingness or capability

I would—implies an expectation

These verbs fulfill the employer's need to know that the applicant is interested in meeting the employer's needs.

Two Verbs to Avoid Using in the Interview Along With "I"

I want—implies a personal desire, wish, requirement, or need

I need—implies personal want

Both of these verbs suggest the job seeker is concerned in advancing his or her own agenda, ignoring the employer's needs.

Phrases to Use in an Interview

added significant telecommunications

adept at conceptualizing "common sense" solutions

broad experience with domestic and global corporations

developed six management candidates

exceed aggressive financial goals

increased check-in efficiency and guest satisfaction

one of my key strengths

produce innovative solutions

proven record of accomplishment

reduced hold time

set an all-time sales record

skilled at analyzing complex business issues

stimulated sales in a stagnant rental market

take the lead

thrive on challenges

transform conceptual ideas into successful events

versatile general manager

willing to take risks

Nonverbal Communications

Before you even open your mouth to speak, you set the tone of the interview by how you look and how you project yourself. Your voice, facial expressions, use of eye contact, and personal appearance all convey a nonverbal message. Your body language sends a message to the interviewer, and research tells us that nonverbal messages carry a far greater impact than the words we speak. If your verbal and nonverbal messages conflict, the nonverbal will more likely be accepted and recognized.

Ten Steps to Confident Body Language

- STEP 1: Enter the room with confidence and enthusiasm, your back straight and your head held high.
- STEP 2: Forget those weak and limp handshakes. Extend your hand to the interviewer and give a firm handshake.

Tip: Avoid those bone-crushing handshakes. You don't want to make a "painful" impression.

- STEP 3: Sit up straight and use good posture throughout the interview.
- STEP 4: Choose a seat close to the interviewer.
- STEP 5: Position your body toward the interviewer and sit with your legs planted firmly on the floor. Avoid fidgeting. Keep your hands relaxed in your lap.
- STEP 6: Make eye contact throughout the interview. Smile often, when appropriate.
- STEP 7: Modulate your voice and speak clearly, maintaining a voice volume that demonstrates self-confidence.
- STEP 8: Pause to gather your thoughts before responding to questions. Avoid clearing your throat prior to speaking.
- STEP 9: Listen attentively to the interviewer, making mental notes of what he or she is looking for.
- STEP 10: Demonstrate your listening skills by integrating information throughout the interview that corresponds to the job requirements provided by the interviewer.

Appearance

Appearance is key in creating that all-important first impression. Your goal is not to direct attention to yourself but to fit the company's image. This can be perplexing with the shift towards casual dress in many organizations.

Tip: Don't rely on the interviewer to forewarn you. When scheduling your interview, ask "What is the dress code" and you'll learn if it is casual business attire or professional business attire. If there is any question, dress in professional business attire.

- STEP 1: Dress in attire appropriate for the job. If you can't get a response from the interviewer, check with the human resources department.

- STEP 2: Don't wear something new; choose a professional and appropriate outfit from your wardrobe that makes you feel confident.

Tip: If your wardrobe lacks something appropriate, purchase the necessary items and then break them in so you'll feel comfortable during the interview process.

- STEP 3: Choose clothing that fits properly, is the correct length, and a current style. You don't want to draw attention for the wrong reasons.
- STEP 4: Good grooming is essential. Have clean and trimmed hair, fingernails, and facial hair for men; no chipped polish for women.
- STEP 5: Ensure that shoes are polished and in good repair, socks match, and hosiery is conservative with no runs.
- STEP 6: Keep cologne or perfume minimal; many individuals have allergies to strong perfume odors.
- STEP 7: Strive for moderation in jewelry and make-up.
- STEP 8: Limit yourself to one or two pairs of earrings; it is prudent to remove earrings from other facial parts.
- STEP 9: Don't fiddle with your hair, tap a pen, or crack your knuckles.
- STEP 10: Practice good dental hygiene.

Tip: Don't chew gum or smoke.

PROFESSIONAL BUSINESS ATTIRE

- Clean and pressed suit, dress shirt, a tie, dress shoes, and appropriate hosiery for men.
- Suit, skirt and jacket, or dress, dress shoes, and hosiery for women.

CASUAL BUSINESS ATTIRE

- Quality sport shirt (no logos), good pair of slacks, often a sports jacket, and good shoes (not boat shoes) for men.

- Quality slacks and tailored shirt, sweater set, or matching jacket and slacks and quality flats for women.

Tip: If your research turns up a dress code of jeans, shorts, and sandals, ask specifics on how you should dress for your meeting.

Practice Makes Perfect

We develop skills through repetition and the best way to master the interview is to practice all the techniques and tips outlined in the previous interview chapters.

Feedback is essential to performance improvement and you'll see first hand how interviewers see you if you videotape your participation in a practice interview. You'll observe your posture, tone of voice, appearance, gestures, and hear how you handle a variety of questions. Be prepared with: video camera; videotape; colleague, friend, or relative to conduct the interview; and tripod for the camera or someone to tape.

- STEP 1: Create an interview environment with two chairs placed together.
- STEP 2: Select a series of questions for the interviewer.
- STEP 3: Brief the interviewer on his or her role.
- STEP 4: Begin taping and conduct a mock interview from the initial greeting through the close.
- STEP 5: Replay the tape and evaluate your nonverbal communication, appearance, and response to questions.
- STEP 6: Identify areas for improvement and practice the corrections.
- STEP 7: Tape the interview again and focus on improving your interview technique.

Tip: Share the tape with someone you trust and ask for feedback and suggestions.

Concluding Your Job Search Successfully

17

Self-Test Your Savvy in Concluding Your Job Search: How Good Are You at Finalizing the Interview Process?

The following self-test is a tool to help you assess whether you are ready to finalize your job search. The objective is not to get the highest score possible, but to pinpoint areas that you can strengthen to help you pursue jobs that interest you through the post-interview phase.

1. Every job seeker should be prepared to negotiate.   T/F __
2. I should follow up every interview, whether I am interested or not, with either a thank-you letter or a phone call.   T/F __
3. All offers should be in writing.   T/F __
4. I should use a job offer as leverage with my existing employer.   T/F __
5. It's advantageous to negotiate benefits when negotiating salary.   T/F __
6. The call should be short when phoning to follow-up on an interview.   T/F __
7. If I bomb on the interview, I should just write it off as experience.   T/F __
8. My thank-you notes should be handwritten.   T/F __
9. I must thoroughly research salaries in my occupation.   T/F __

10. If I was really interested and not offered a position, I should call the interviewer and ask what I can do better next time to get another position.   T/F __

11. It's possible to salvage an interview that didn't go well.   T/F __

12. All salaries are negotiable.   T/F __

13. Organizations will rarely negotiate benefits.   T/F __

14. I should give full attention during salary negotiations and not take notes.   T/F __

15. I can quit my job as soon as I get an offer.   T/F __

16. Each salary survey provides different information so I should use more than one when researching salaries.   T/F __

17. I can go back to an interviewer after the interview to clarify or expand on a question.   T/F __

18. I should never leave a voice mail message when placing a phone call after the interview.   T/F __

19. The best way to research salaries is online.   T/F __

20. Thank-you letters should be written within 24 hours of the interview.   T/F __

21. Job seekers frequently send thank-you letters after interviews.   T/F __

Total: _____

Score 1 point for each "True" response and 0 for each "False" response, EXCEPT for questions 4, 7, 8, 12, 13, 14, 15, 18, 19, 21. *For these questions only*, **subtract** 1 point for each "True" response. Record your total. A score below +9 indicates that you would benefit from practicing the interview techniques discussed in this chapter. (*Note:* It is possible to have a negative score.)

Post-Interview Fundamentals

Most interviews end without an offer, so you'll need to use a variety of post-interview techniques to culminate your search successfully. Some of these topics have been covered in earlier chapters, but I have organized them together with additional strategies that will lead you through this final phase and help you secure the all-important job offer.

Thank-You Letters

The interview doesn't end when you walk out the door. If you are interested in the job, follow up with a thank-you letter, a phone call, or both. Your goal is to zero in on professional details that make you uniquely qualified.

A thank-you letter or note is an opportunity to demonstrate courtesy and your ability to communicate in writing. It should be sent quickly, within 24 hours, for maximum effect.

Thank-you letters and notes can make the difference between consideration or refusal—and yet many job seekers fail to use this powerful tool. Effective letters and notes must:

Be personal.

Convey your enthusiasm for the position.

Reinforce your credentials.

Be grammatically correct.

Be effectively written.

For more information on thank-you letters, check out Chapter 10.

Phone Calls

It is always appropriate to follow up an interview with a phone call. The purpose of the call is to thank the interviewer for his or her time and reaffirm your interest in the position. The phone call should be short, a reminder, and not an intrusion. Never make a pest of yourself.

Phone calls aren't easy to make, so consider preparing a script. You will be more relaxed if you know in advance what you want to say. Here's an example you can modify to meet your needs.

YOUR SCRIPT: HOW TO FOLLOW UP AN INTERVIEW

"Hello, Ms. White. This is Robbie Kaplan. I wanted to follow up on our interview last week and let you know how interested I am in the ** position."

(Pause; give her a chance to respond.)

"I'm intrigued with the new product slated for July launch and I have some ideas for the marketing campaign."

(Pause; give her a chance to respond.)

"Can you tell me when you'll be making a decision for the ** position?"

(Pause.)

"I look forward to hearing from you. Thanks again for all your time."

If you're having trouble reaching your contact, keep trying. Here are some suggestions for making contact:

- Try calling between 8:00 and 8:30 in the morning or between 5:00 and 6:00 in the evening. Those may be the best times to catch your contact in his or her office.

- Continue calling for a day or two if you're getting voice mail, eventually leaving a message that you wanted to speak with him or her personally, couldn't catch him or her, and then leave a short message.

- If the recipient's calls are being screened, either state you will call back or leave a message.

- If all else fails and you have the person's electronic mail address, send an electronic letter (see Chapter 6).

Tips on Negotiating Salary and Benefits

Congratulations, you've been offered the job! You have handled your search well, but don't lose focus on finalizing the offer and the search in your excitement.

If you are like most people, you probably find salary negotiations difficult, but it is a skill well worth learning.

It's important to remember the purpose and process of negotiation; your ultimate goal is to come to an agreement on salary and benefits that satisfies both you and the employer. Avoid beginning a new job where either you or the employer is the clear winner, as one of you will not be happy.

1. Do your homework; find out exactly what you should be making and what the position pays.
2. Plan your expectations; determine what you want in the way of salary and benefits.
3. Identify non-negotiable items; for example, vacation benefits comparable to what you are currently receiving.
4. Determine the minimum salary and benefits to which you will agree.
5. Know the employer's interests; it will be useful to get an insider perspective on the organization's salary structure, goals, and limitations.

Tip: Be flexible and adaptable without losing sight of your salary and benefit expectations.

If you don't do your research and neglect to negotiate the best and most appropriate salary, it will be extremely difficult for you to catch up to others in comparable positions who are being paid more. Most jobs have salary ranges—starting, mid-point, and maximum. A particular job may have several salary ranges, depending on whether the position is entry- or senior-level. You must know the range of the salary and what your skills, experience, training, and education are worth in the workplace.

Tip: You cannot always negotiate salary. Many positions in the public sector and with unions are non-negotiable.

Researching Salaries

You must thoroughly investigate salaries for your occupation and know what your job is worth in the marketplace.

- STEP 1: Locate salary surveys that identify salary ranges from professional and trade associations, executive search firms, employment agencies, federal and state government agencies, and on the Internet. Business and professionally-oriented magazines, newspapers, and trade publications publish annual salary surveys. Access additional information through newspaper employment listings, job postings, Internet Web sites, and technical/trade journals.

- STEP 2: Access the following Internet resources: **Bureau of Labor Statistics (www.stats.bls.gov)** provides annual surveys of salary statistics based on hourly rates and key cities/states. **WageWeb (www.wageweb.com)** provides annual salary information based on 2,080 working hours in a year for over 160 administrative, finance, information management, engineering, health-care, sales, marketing, and manufacturing positions. **Salary.com (www.salary.com)** offers diverse salary information from reports to articles.

- STEP 3: Request occupational salary information from colleagues, professional networks, friends, and human resources departments.

- STEP 4: Contact the career center where you attended college or your local colleges. They often keep statistics on placements and salaries.

- STEP 5: Be direct and call the organization and request the salary range for the position.

- STEP 6: Establish your current salary with incentives and then use the salary information you've gathered to determine the salary you are making, the one you would like, and the lowest amount you are willing to accept.

- STEP 7: Benefit plans now come in all shapes and sizes. Identify what benefits the position offers including health, insurance, retirement contribution, stock options, vacation, holidays, training, transportation subsidy, and tuition reimbursement. Both salary and benefits are often negotiable. If you don't need the health coverage, you may be able to negotiate a higher salary or retirement contribution. Determine your needs and desires prior to negotiation.

- STEP 8: Document your salary research.
- STEP 9: Prepare a statement on your salary request and justification.
- STEP 10: Take your writing portfolio to the salary negotiations to record information during the salary and benefit negotiation process.

Ten Questions to Ask and Issues to Discuss When Negotiating Salary

1. "I'm currently making $xx and I'd like to jump to $zz. Can your organization support that?"

Tip: Be prepared to support why you should be earning more.

---

2. "I have been making $xx and I think I am worth $zz in the job we are discussing."
3. "My last salary increase was nine months ago and I think we should consider that in the offer."
4. "Your scheduled salary increase plan provides for increases at what interval?"
5. "What were the average salary increases last year?"
6. "Is there opportunity to earn performance-based bonuses?"
7. "What is the salary expectation for the next logical career step for me in your organization?"
8. "How long do you expect it would take for someone with my skills to get there?"
9. "How much of my regular salary increase will be based on personal performance?"
10. "How much will be based on organizational performance?"

Post-Interview Assessment

Interviewing is a skill. You are not born with skills; rather they are developed and learned—and expertise is gained by studying and practicing.

Improve your interviewing skills by conducting a post-interview assessment that identifies your strengths and potential areas for improvement. Evaluate:

> Areas where you were prepared
>
> Areas where you were unprepared
>
> The appropriateness of your dress
>
> Specific questions you handled well
>
> Questions you were unprepared to answer
>
> How you can improve
>
> Areas requiring follow-up

Tips to Salvage a Shaky Interview

You may be perfectly qualified, your experience a true match, but you just know when you leave the interview that it didn't go well. How you follow up will make the difference between disappointment or an offer.

1. Contact the interviewer immediately and confirm if he or she also felt the meeting did not go well.
2. State very straightforwardly what it is that wasn't emphasized, covered in the interview, or misconstrued. For example: "I sensed we were not both convinced this was a good fit. Here's what I think we missed. . . ."
3. Compose a follow-up letter addressing any question or issue you felt lacked an effective response. (See Chapter 11).
4. Network to find someone who knows someone in the organization who can put in a good word for you.
5. Think of some questions to ask to give yourself the opportunity to speak with someone again, either in person or by phone.

6. Alert your references to address your strengths or experiences in the area of concern.
7. Solicit feedback from the interviewer and use the information to reinforce your candidacy.
8. If you are not offered the position, ask how you can improve your skills for the next interview or enhance your credentials so you will ace the next opportunity.

Tip: It makes sense to maintain cordial relations with prospective employers and express your continued interest. You may have been the hiring manager's next choice and when another opportunity occurs, you get the offer.

Tendering Your Resignation

It is imperative that you carefully handle this final step in the job search process. You must have a written offer in hand before you resign to protect yourself should the offer fall through at the last minute. A verbal offer is not the final offer; you must have a written offer detailing salary, benefits, start date, and any negotiated employment details.

You may speak to your supervisor in person when you have the offer letter in hand and follow up with a resignation letter. Or, prepare your resignation letter, using Chapter 13, and either deliver it in person or through the interoffice mail or postal service.

Résumé Index
by Occupation

Index